THE GREAT "BEING"

CREATOR, YAHWEH, ALLAH, GOD

Gwinyai H. Muzorewa

Wipf and Stock Publishers
EUGENE, OREGON

Wipf and Stock Publishers
199 West 8th Avenue, Suite 3
Eugene, Oregon 97401

The Great Being: Creator, Yahweh, Chuku, Allah, God, Brahman
An Introduction to the World's Major Religions
By Muzorewa, Gwinyai H.
Copyright©2000 Muzorewa, Gwinyai H.
ISBN: 1-57910-453-3
Publication date: August, 2000
Previously published by , 2000.

Contents

Acknowledgments — v

Introduction — vii

Chapter 1 - What is Religion? Or, Why Religion? — 1
    Religion and Magic
    Categories of Religion
    Personalities
    True Religion and Related Characteristics
    Does God Exist?

Chapter 2 - African Traditional Religion — 21
    The Hierarchy of Beings in African Cosmology
    The Concept of God
    The Concept of Ancestry
    The Concepts of Good and Evil
    Mythology and Morality in African Religion
    The Concept of Humanity in Community
    Humanity and Morality
    Summary

Chapter 3 - Hinduism — 41
    General Introduction
    Religions of India

    Hindu Worldview
    Hinduism and its Sacred Scriptures
    The Origins and Development of Hinduism
    The Caste System
    Salvation in Most Religions in General
    Salvation in Hinduism (in particular)
    The Role and Function of the Guru

Chapter 4 - Buddhism   59
    The Life of Founder
    The Great Enlightenment
    The Four Noble Truths
    The Self
    The Concept of Karma
    Compassion and Wisdom
    Buddhism: Development After the Founder's Death
    Some Commonalities and Differences (between Theravadins
        and Mahayanists)

Chapter 5 - Taoism   70
    Taoist Beliefs
    The Taoist Cosmos
    Divinities
    The Nature of Humanity
    Taoist Practice and Morality (Ethics)

Chapter 6 - Judaism   76
    The Rise of Judaism: An Overview
    The Patriarchs and the Covenant
    Divine Deliverance
    Kosher Laws
    Obedience to the Torah

Chapter 7 - Christianity   87
    The Background of Christianity
    The Life of the Founder
    The Distinguishing Character of the Founder
    Salient Christian Beliefs
    Christian Doctrine of Humanity
    The Immorality of the Soul
    Christian Faith and Practice

Chapter 8 - Islam   101

    General Background
    The Founder of Islam: Muhammad
    Organization and Institutions
    Islamic Theology
    Islamic Law

ACKNOWLEDGMENTS

Several factors have necessitated the writing of this book on "Introduction to some of the Major Religions of the World." What pressured me most to put this book together is the fact that since my teens, it always made me not only wonder, but also angry to note that every book on major religions of the world made the intentional error of omitting one of the oldest and major religions of the world, namely African religion - the religion of the first human community on Earth! I always wanted to see the African religion included, in fact, regarded as the very first! So I thank all the authors who either omitted or mentioned "in passing" the religion that initially worshiped the *Great Spirit God*. If many scholars had written a chapter or two on this pristine religion, I might not have been inspired to do this work.

Secondly, I wish to thank my wife, Sue, who always encourages me to do what I ought to do - namely, put "those thoughts on paper, Gwinyai!" So now I have some peace of mind, at least so far, because I have done what I know I "ought to do."

Thirdly, I thank Lincoln University's secretariat; specifically, the Religion Department Secretary, who worked hard to give this book its initial form. Also, Ms. Denise Williamson, who worked after hours and weekends to prepare the camera-ready copy for publication, deserves glory and honor.

But most of all, I always give thanks to that Great Spirit God, who gives me every single breath to breathe, in my sleep and in my wake hours. Only God is worthy to be praised!

Teaching the "Introduction to Religions of the World" has given me the rare exposure to most of these important spiritual traditions whose main single function is to inject morality into every human culture. Though they each claim the first place, me thinks they all deserve appreciation.

I take responsibility for all mistakes in this book because I had all the help I needed to produce a reasonable introductory account of the few religions I have addressed here. At the same time, I have to apologize to any religious tradition which I may have unintentionally misrepresented. Such errors are often the result of a plethora of sources on the market today. Further, it is not uncommon that one religion may have more than a single perspective, resulting in a theological diversity.

Introduction

The study of the major religions of the world is expected to enlighten anyone who takes the subject seriously because, ideally, one has to understand each tradition as presented by its own adherents. A study of "religions" is not the same as a comparative study of religions, which tends to focus on "comparison." Our approach in this introductory survey is one that seeks to understand each tradition as it is - values, doctrine, concepts and praxis.

We note here that it is not our intention to go to great length trying to justify the inclusion of African religion in this brief introduction. We, however, need to point out that this religion represents the oldest spiritual traditions in human history. If we date Hinduism or Judaism as far back as 65000-15000 B.C.E.., we must remind ourselves that African religion may have begun over two million years ago since religion, for the Africans, is a way of life - not a ritual set aside for special days and hour of the day. Neither is "prayer" said five times a day! African life is African religion and African religion is African life. The two are inseparable. It follows, too, that the idea of atheism is totally foreign to traditional Africa. No matter how much a person is estranged from the Great Spirit God, it remains a case of "estrangement," implying distancing oneself from the Reality which one *knows* to exist and to be the Ultimate.

Because African religion is probably the oldest, as we have already stated, and has always been an oral tradition, it is not possible to identify the individual founder. What is certain is that this religion has always worshiped the true Living God - the Creator of not only the various galaxies, but all the species of the world, including human beings. It is, therefore, not by chance that this book discusses African religion before any others. Also, the title of this book: *"The Great Being: Creator, Yahweh, Allah, God,"* is intended to portray the basic African belief that

"God is Being" and those who seek to worship God must do so in Spirit and in Truth.

We also have to point out in this introduction that most informed scholars of African religion concur that from the dawn of the African religion, idol worship was never an option for the African. Even when white Euro-American missionaries tried to "create idol worship" for Africans by alleging that Africans worship their ancestors, that idea never took hold because African ancestors are mere human spirits/souls created by the Great Being and *ipsofacto* do not qualify to be worshiped. Ancestors have their particular role in traditional Africa: they are the object of veneration. Every child must be cultured enough to "honor [your] father and mother." This is part of what it is to be an African.

From the traditional names of God among African peoples, any etymologist can tell that such names depict a "Great Being" who has a distinct place in the Universe. God is God! God is not like any other beings; in fact, God is that vital force that brought into existence all other beings. God is *aseity* - self-existent!

Now to present the format and sequence of chapters, we draw the reader's attention to the contents of Chapter 1 because almost every religion is likely to have aspects if not all of the components discussed in this first chapter. For my students, particular attention should be paid to the section on "chief characteristics" of major religions. Of course, we are aware that if a group of people - even hate groups - could make an effort to incorporate these "characteristics," their experience will always abort at the point of Divine Presence which cannot be faked. True religion is not humanity's figment of its imagination.

What we have in this book is a skeletal presentation of facts and beliefs of each of the religions included here. The author has made an effort to make the rise of each religion fairly clear, but time and space during the semester do not allow an in-depth discussion of several issues that arise in the process. Also, the author could not describe each religion and trace its presence to the present day for the same reason - time and space. However and therefore, the student will be encouraged to develop a research topic that leads him or her to examine current issues and/or status of any religion of one's choice. For instance, the student may want to "trace" the presence of Jews in Africa, or the political influence of Islam in African Colonial Administration, or the impact of Eastern religions on the West, and so forth. The professor is encouraged to help students choose topics outside this text in terms of contents but within the purview of religions introduced in this textbook.

Chapter 1

What is Religion? Or, Why Religion?

Religions, as we define the term here, are characterized by certain phenomena. The most paramount feature among many religions is a component that "moves" humanity to the depths of the human sublime. At the core of human ontology, there is a spiritual feeling which triggers the "religious consciousness" of an individual, prompting him or her to seek a Higher Being or Ideal believed to assure the individual some sense of security or immortality and enlightenment. When this occurs, one finds himself or herself renouncing certain pleasures in order to attain this most desired goal. It is important to note that one forsakes such pleasures voluntarily. If it means one has to assume a given form of burdens in order to accomplish this noble goal, one will commit oneself to do so. Indeed what we are attempting to capture in words here refuses to be "boxed," taking after the nature of the Ultimate Reality. All we can do here is give a hint.

Religion is a powerful, if not forceful feeling, with a mysterious motivating energy. Though this subject is spiritual, we can still use the term "science of religion" if we define science as knowledge. Religion is intended to teach us to know mystery as mystery. In fact, individuals and communities have fought wars for the sake of religion. Some people have been crucified for the sake of their religion. Some have been burned on the stake for the sake of their faith; others have been tortured (thrown into a lake of fire or a den of lions) for the sake of their spiritual beliefs. Many will agree that religious beliefs constitute a very costly commodity. But knowledge is not enough. Religion is also an experience of the knowledge as well as gnosis and manifestation of what one may have experienced.

At the same time one must note that, in most cases, those who inflict "punishment," ranging from acts as severe as excommunicating one or hundreds of thousands of believers to actually murdering, do so in the name of their own religion! When one realizes the seriousness with which religion is guarded or attacked, it becomes apparent that religions must be one of the major concerns of humanity. It is no wonder religion is one of the most controversial and sensitive general topics (others being sex and politics).

One reason religion is such an important subject is that it governs humanity's whole being. What is strange about the whole issue of religion, however, is that - strictly speaking - religion does not originate within the heart or mind of the human being. Rather, at its very best, religion has external spiritual origins. Humanity internalizes religion to such a degree that it appears as if the origin of religion is the human soul. In fact, it is for this reason that some opponents of religion (atheists) have contended that religion is a figment of the human mind. They arrived at this erroneous conclusion because they could not understand how an external force (entity, power and influence) could control the human mind or heart that, for example, an adherent may be willing to die for his or her religion!

Careful reflection on the subject indicates that what actually happens is that the human soul - at its very depths - is touched and moved by an external power. Obviously, this external reality must be peculiar. It cannot be just an ordinary phenomenon or else it could not strike the human imagination so much. Yet, its peculiarity must be such that it draws the human soul to itself as objects that belong together. Put differently, there is a degree of "likeness" which compels the soul to struggle, even dangerously, for the sake of "being in communion" with this other being. This is especially the case where the religion in question believes in God, not just a higher ideal. But, even in the case of belief in a higher ideal, that ideal must be such that it promises or assures the adherent quality life which is most desirable - something worth identifying with eternally. Part of the religious sentiments comes from the inherent desire for immortality. Even a poor, suffering person hopes to live forever "in that perfect world." Religion also gives a sense of belonging. Thus, religion can be summarized as human response to Divine, or Higher Ideal.

"Holiness" or "wholly otherness" is another element of the mystery involved in the relationship between the "holy" and the "secular" (or unholy). There is a fascinating attraction between God and humanity which is only holy when sanctified by God, the source of sacredness.

Further, Christians believe that the death of a religious person who lives in relation with God and God's holiness, is peculiar. Such death is different from ordinary death because, as in the case of the Christian religion, this death is in fact the foundation and pre-requisite for eternal life. But the Christian religion is not the only one that attributes rich meaning to death. Christianity offers a good example because in Jesus Christ, death is presented as the will of God, who also has power over the sting of death. This is demonstrated by Jesus' resurrection - victory over death!

All religions must experience some form or sense of "holiness." Most religions actually have "holy literature" (a sacred book) which serves to describe what holiness is and is about. There is a sense in which the concept of holiness is synonymous with that of religion. Differently put, just as one cannot think of ethics without the concept of goodness or morality, one cannot conceive of religion without some concept of holiness. Furthermore, once the adherent has sensed holiness, the next move is to devise ritualistic acts of worship as ways to manifest adoration. This is triggered by the juxtaposition of "holy" and the "secular." Consequently, it is logical to surmise that worshiping the holy seems to be "making up" for the difference between the two realities (i.e., the sacred and the profane). In most cases, the Divine makes itself known and then requires acts of adoration. Religion is response to Divine initiative.

In more advanced spiritual communities, the gap between the sacred and the profane closes up because that which is profane has developed an inseparable relationship with that which is sacred, and vice versa. True, the sacred and the profane are not the same, but they live as though they belong together. Again, the Christian religion gives us a good example of this: the Son of God (Jesus Christ) is believed to be both divine and human. In Jesus, humanity and divinity connect for the purpose of consolidating and theologically reconciling this Divine-Human relationship. Therefore, the idea of the "Holy" is at once both "wholly other" and "inseparably in union with." This characteristic creates a special bond between religion and the human soul. The soul will not rest until it finds rest in the object of religion. And the gods in most religions, eternally seek to save the soul while the latter seeks to appease God in order to be secure forever!

Put differently, holiness is always experienced as a dual feeling - frightening and delightful - setting apart from and attracting all to itself. Humanity finds in it the fulfillment of its longings. Simultaneously, humanity feels judged "adversely" by the presence of the holy. Holiness can also be best described as the "numinous."

There is incredible power in holiness - power that frightens humanity. In the Christian bible the statement, "the fear of the Lord is the beginning of wisdom," expresses best what we are trying to explain here. Incidentally this "fear" is not negative! It would be erroneous to surmise that the idea of God originated from this fear. This "fear" is not the same as "phobia." Furthermore, the fear of the Lord is different from fear of the unknown. The fear of the Lord means knowing "first things first," it means sound judgment.

Holiness is experienced in various forms and contexts. Many religions regard certain objects, as well as places, as sacred. Deities are regarded as holy, but so are their places of habitation; e.g., the sky, the trees, the altars, the temples, the mountains and caves. In addition to these, persons who serve the gods are also regarded as holy: prophets, priests, the Shaman, and even magicians. Also, certain ritual acts and words are regarded as scared; e.g. sacrifice, words, signs, images and so forth, as long as they are closely associated with gods. Holiness is power because of its quality of otherness, superiority, sublimity, absoluteness and mystery. Holiness escapes comprehension, yet gods want to be understood, pleased and adored because they are holy. Holiness is a power with which to be reckoned. Holiness is a commodity with its own power and authority.

Depending on a people's level of maturity, holiness seems to summarize the idea of religion. It is our estimation in this book that the concept of holiness is probably more essential than the notion of deity in the minds of many. People can belong to a religion even when their understanding of their god is vague, but they are sure to know the distinction between the holy and the profane. Indeed, one might say an idea of God, void of the concept of the holy, lacks what makes religion what it is. Put differently, there can be no true religion without the idea of the numinous. At the center of religion, there is the power, the numinous, the mystery, the holy, the supernatural, sacredness, and God.

Religion and Magic

There has been an unfortunate connection between magic and religion, probably because magic is believed to be "beyond reason," as religion is conceived of as being supernatural in most cases. In this book where religion is presented as a science, religion cannot be viewed as magic whatsoever! Simply put, magic has nothing to do with religion.

Understood as peoples' vain attempt to reverse the principles of causality, magic is an effort to practice "science," to do the impossible through certain powers which "no one can explain" except the magician himself or herself. Magic is an attempt to direct "natural forces." Some people have, in fact, advanced the theory that religion is the second phase of magic in the sense that humanity struggles vainly to control natural forces. Now, through religion, the power to control is left up to the gods. All humanity has to do is "pray" (or ask) the gods to do "the impossible."

Unfortunately, this theory cannot be accepted in the light of the history of religions, which clearly indicates other reasons for the origins of religions. At its best, magic is the appearance of ability to "harness supernatural secrets." It is an attempt to reduce supernatural secrets to a profane power. While the believer venerates supernatural secrets, the magician equips himself or herself with these and employs them, often to his/her glory. In fact, understanding this distinction helps us to differentiate the two: in religion, humanity seeks to venerate deity, whereas the magician makes every effort, though vainly, to coerce the divine principle for his or her own purposes. Furthermore, whereas in religion (especially god-centered religions) the deity is the master, in magic the magician is. Neither does magic confine itself to things material. It also purports to deal with spiritual powers. The magician uses gods just as other items employed to accomplish his/her own purpose. To summarize, where religion worships God, magicians use divine secrets to their own end. Thus it is fair to say magic is "human-centered" whereas religion is "God-centered."

Note that throughout the history of religions, there have been incidences where religious people have tended to use religion as magic. In the age of television evangelism, the preachers occasionally present Christian religion as "magic" in order to draw crowds, yet religion and magic are magnitudes of different qualities. The essence of religion is a feeling of dependence on the creator; a feeling of absolute trusting surrender; reverence to God. In the true sense, religion begins when humanity feels totally inadequate in the face of a power that fills humanity with a sense of awe and reverence. Religion comes to life when the individual has had the courage to take a good look at himself or herself and realize one's own inadequacies, faults, and limitations in the presence of the powerful, the numinous, the omniscient, the creator of the universe, who can empower humanity. On the other hand, magic consists of unfounded self-glorification, an element of megalomania. Magic is more of an ideology, where religion is more of a theology.

This discussion is incomplete until the observation has been made that no matter how "similar" religion and magic may be in certain aspects; and no matter how eloquently one may argue that magic is the origin of religion; the two have no common origin, neither are their goals the same.

The history of particular religions whose origin is *revelation*, such as Islam, Judaism and Christianity, has been the story of the liberation of a people initiated by the creator of humanity. Revelation generally presupposes external initiative - meaning that there is a Being or Force out there that seeks to transform a given community by calling that people to higher goals - even eternal living. Thus, in religion, humanity encounters a power that is far superior to humanity, calling humanity to a better life and this in communion with God - bringing together the holy and the profane for the salvation of creation.

Responding to this Divine invitation constitutes the essence of religion.

Although some scholars argue that religion originates and evolves from the concept of magic, the majority agree with our perspective here that the preliminary stage of religion is the Divine call and human response to a meaningful existence - even moral life leading on to the immortality of the soul. Our logic and meaning which leads us to this conclusion is based on the premise that the human soul originates from the Eternal Spirit which has always been in existence. To the school of thought that believes that there is a co-relation between religion and magic, one reminds them that at best magic is a human attempt to emulate a divine being, which is the essence of religion. Furthermore, magicians look to humanity as the source of power while religionists look up to God or Supreme Reality as the source of power.

To sum, magic is more like science without proof than anything else. Magic is similar to science in that its results are purely the work of the human mind, whereas such is not the case with religion, which is God-centered. The difference between science and magic is that science seeks to "show" its method through proofs and experiments, whereas magic seeks to show only its "results" and struggles to conceal its method.

Categories of Religions

To further deepen our understanding of religions - from the definition to the phenomenon - it is instructive to classify them into categories based on certain criteria. For instance, one may group religions into three: (1) nature religions, (2) folk religions, and (3) world religions.

Nature religions refer to the religions of the so-called primitive peoples who are wise enough to realize that their life is dependent on harmony with everything else that the Creator has brought into being. They know that to "honor" nature is to respect and appreciate the Creator! It is unfortunate that these religions have been designated as "polytheistic" by those who do not understand how they function. To those who comprehend them, it is clear that all aspects of religion ultimately seek "to worship" the Supreme Reality and to promote congenial community. Scholars of the so-called advanced religions should know that just because nature religions have so many altars and what appears as "objects of worship," does not mean lack of understanding of the Ultimate Truth. It may actually connote the opposite.

Folk religions refer to the religions of many "civilized nations." Their gods represent natural cosmic forces, which are believed to guarantee human existence. To this category belong the religions of Greece, Rome, Babylon, Egypt, ancient India and ancient China, and the ancient Germanic peoples, according to Hans-Joachim Shoeps (*1968, 49*).

The third category is **World religions**. These are different from other categories in that they "break out of the cultural and historical limitations of a given community."

Religions may also be classified by contrasting types, based on what is observable. For instance, we can contrast folk religions with world religions; revelational religions with natural; primitive religions with advanced religions. Founded religions may also be contrasted with unfounded religions. However, this is not our task here.

Personalities

Almost all major religions share the presence of the following personalities who play principle roles in not only the founding and doctrines but also the functioning of these religions: the founders, the prophets, the priests, the mystics and, almost invariably, the reformers (and sometimes a counter reformer!). Of course, above these is assumed the presence of a God, some High Ideal, or Supreme Reality or Ultimate Truth.

While every religion can be traced to an original source, many have a single individual who is regarded as the founder. Good examples of such religions are Christianity which was founded by Jesus Christ who, himself, was an active member and adherent of Judaism; Muhammad founder of Islam, belonged to Christianity. One cannot really generalize how religions are founded because of various circumstances surrounding each incident. But one could argue with reasonable credibility that for one to be the founder of a religion, one must possess a certain amount of charisma - something about the individual's personality that draws people to him or her. This could even be posthumously. Often times when the founder is born he or she may grow up an ordinary person until something "clicks"! Some founders are "called" by Divinity from their respective "secular professions or careers." Others are "called from the womb of their mothers." In each case, there is always a critical *moment of consciousness*. In this respect, I agree with the view that, in most cases, "the founder is the witness of revelation." The founder **experiences** or **hears** a message and the rest of the adherents follow him or her on the strength of one's charisma and credibility. To avoid abstraction, allow me to cite a classical example of how a religion is established by an ordinary person who becomes the *founder*!

When Moses was in the field, looking after his father-in-law's livestock, he had (saw, heard and believed) what is popularly referred to as the burning bush experience. That contact between an ordinary individual (at least in our eyes, Moses was an ordinary person) and God - Yahweh - (*Exodus Chapter 3*) marked the beginning or founding of the religion now known as Judaism. Of course, there are some people who argue that Abraham is the founder of Judaism. Another glaring example of the founding of a religion is the contact between Muhammed and Allah (through Gabriel, the Angel of the Lord). Again, an ordinary person is "called." Typically, he experienced the revelation and his witness to the world resulted in the religion known today as Islam. Characteristic of each instance, in the case of the majority of the Middle East crescent religions God speaks or calls, and the would-be founder **listens, hears,** and **responds**.... This sequence of events confirms the theology that "religion is humanity's response to God's call." God takes the *initiative*! Christianity, Judaism and Islam have the answer to the anticipated question: namely, why does God take the initiative? The answer is simple, yet profound. God loves humanity, Allah is compassionate! Clearly, this view dispels the theory that religion is the figment of humanity's imagination. Rather it is an organized response to Divine initiative.

Furthermore, it is common that founders of religions become venerated by the adherents. With exceptions like Moses, we cannot say veneration is the rule, but we observe that such is the tendency.

Gautama actually told his people not to worship him. Muhammed also makes his position clear. "I am not Allah. I am only the last prophet." In spite of these efforts, "we find a cult of the founders in Christianity, Buddhism, Muhammadism, Zaroastrianism, Manichaeism, Confucianism and Taoism" (*Hans Joachim Schoeps 1968, 41*).

In addition to charisma, there tends to develop a legend surrounding the founder's birth. People begin to "remember" how circumstances surrounding the birth of the founder were supernatural. For example, Mary, the mother of Jesus, experienced supernatural visits from angels from the time she conceived until she had to run away with the baby to safety. Queen Mahamaya also experienced "strange" events during her pregnancy with Gautama - the Buddha.

Other rather common features are: the temptations of these founders by Satan, transfiguration of these people, and miracles surrounding the death of the founder. Among these we note that Christianity has an extreme case because it is the only one that claims that after its founder was killed, dead for three days, God raised him again. However, if we look beyond materialism, most of us would agree that the bottom line is the fact that the *founders* (or at least their spirits) are believed to live *eternally*. Each situation confirms the theology of the immortality of the *soul*.

Almost every founder has a mission to his people, if not to the world. Although people tend to turn around and worship these founders, the **call** is for all to receive the message of **truth**. There was a time when I sympathized with those who tend to get preoccupied with the question, "which 'truth' shall we listen to?" I have since resolved that (and many religions concur) *truth* is one. Each religion employs its own method believing that "their method" is the most effective. The substance earlier in this chapter substantiates this position where we tabulate values of most religions and characteristics of the major religions of the world. Also, the last chapter in this book is intended to direct us toward the possibility of a universal understanding of religion. It is important that religions present the *truth* if they have been commissioned to "preach" the message of salvation, enlightenment and eternal life. Without exception, the life of each founder to date has pointed to a moral, pious, obedient and spiritual goal. The founders have all pointed to the possibility of eternal life beginning in this world.

However, not every religion has an individual as its founder. There are some religions which have arisen from the people. The majority of such religions tend to have a very long tradition. In most cases we can only point to the "fathers" - the patriarchs. Whatever the case, the elements of the revelation of the message *AND* the message relating to the are relationship between humanity and the Ultimate Reality (or Truth), is still embedded in such religions. Although there may be no particular individual who has the charisma to draw adherents together, there is something about the faith itself that draws people together, generation after generation. In fact, there is a sense in which one could argue that the charisma is embedded within the body of beliefs - whether it is written or oral. However, in general, there are certain religious personalities who perform major functions.

a.   The Prophets

Defined as "a person inspired by God to speak the truth in God's name," a prophet is one summoned by God to interpret His message to a people. In Judaism, prophets always prefixed their statements thus: "Thus said the Lord" to signify that what they say is not their own message but that of the Lord God. Again, one may define "prophet' as a "critic of society." If society's morals are against God's will or truth, he or she is a prophet who speaks up against such immorality. Put differently, a prophet is God's mouthpiece. Often times one is called to be a prophet even against one's will, since "to speak the truth" is often risky business. One risks popularity by speaking the truth. One could lose friends by speaking prophetically. But since it is God who calls or appoints the prophet, one has no choice. A prophecy is not just about the future - it is also about the truth today.

For instance, in Judaism Jeremiah tells us how God summoned him to be a prophet in these words (God's words):

> "Before I formed you in the womb I knew you, and before you were born I consecrated you; I appointed you a prophet to the nation" (*Jeremiah Ch. 1*).

Furthermore, God *enables* whomever He appoints to be a prophet. God can give us the ability to do whatever is in the interest of God's people. Again, back to Jeremiah, when he tried to advance excuses, like "I am only a youth; I do not know what to say," God said,

> "Do not say 'I am only a youth' for to all whom I send you, you shall go, and whatever I command you, you shall speak... Behold I have put my word in your mouth" (Jeremiah Ch. 1).

In Jewish tradition, a prophet is not trained to be one - neither does he emerge from tradition. To the contrary, a prophet often comes to "break" the tradition when tradition no longer reflects God's will. God equips the prophet, as we have heard in Jeremiah's case. A prophet is not like a chairperson of some organization. It is apparent that prophets become such under duress of their God. Traditionally, being a prophet was not a career because God sent the prophet to proclaim a particular message, hopefully once, maybe twice.

Prophets play a peculiar role with respect to eschatology. As God's mouthpiece, a prophet can pronounce judgment on anyone based on his or her misdeeds. Israel, as a theocracy, took seriously the prophet's message because they knew that what the prophet uttered would undoubtedly "come to pass" because God does not speak in vain. Religion is an important segment in a society that takes prophetism seriously. Kings were appointed by the prophets; victory or defeat was foreseen by the prophet; national disasters such as hunger, drought or disease were foreseen by the prophet. People could not afford to ignore the word from the prophet's mouth. Today, many who believe in the prophets expect them to prophesy the future, even the end of time; but, as the Black community witnessed in Dr. Martin Luther King, Jr., in the United States, the prophet speaks the truth that can unfold in our time.

b.   The Mystic

The mystic is one who strives for the liberation of the soul from material bondage, in pursuit of union with the Ultimate Reality - God or the highest Ideal. The mystic strives to destroy the ego in order to achieve the apex of ecstatic experience. Mysticism seeks inner perception rather than external perceptions. Mysticism is described as passive, quietistic and only focused on inwardness. It is esoteric, secret and non-proselytizing. It is timeless and ahistorical. Unlike prophetism, which is extremely time-conscious (pending judgment), mysticism is wholly unhistorical. It deals with the concept of timelessness. Mysticism, for instance, would rather "Christ is born in you," not in Bethlehem, which would mean Christ is born every day and not once upon a time. Mysticism treasures the Buddhamind in each one of us, rather than the Buddha who was born 570 BCE. Mystics across all religions tend to share much in common, even though their particular contexts make each case (mystic) different from the rest of the others. Mysticism is indeed a different type of science. It is science (a way of knowing) of its own type.

c. The Priest

A priest is primarily a functionary. He is naturally counterpoised to the laity in his role as a religious leader. The priest is a representative of the community, empowered to watch over the administration of general community worship - and, specifically, the sacrifices. Every religion that makes sacrifices to its god must do so through the institution of the priesthood. It seems that the gods will only acknowledge our offerings and sacrifices if they are presented by the priests. The priests also sometimes serve in a judicial capacity. Whereas the prophet serves to pronounce judgment to the community, the priests serve to transmit the blessing of Yahweh to the community in traditional Judaism and other "traditional" religions such as the African and Native American religions.

In most religions, the priestly office represents the conservative element. For instance, so many other things may change but certain rituals will always be the same for generations and generations. By the way, in some religions the priesthood is hereditary but in others it is conveyed through consecration and laying on of hands. Overall, it is fair to say the priest is antithetical to both the mystic and the prophet. These are "set apart" within the community, but the priest represents the most conservative institution of the community. In African religion, every head of the household functions as a priest at family level.

Every religion has this office (of the priest) although not all religions name them as such. The office is crucial because it represents a critical *link* between the highest Ideal and the masses - between God and the believers.

d. The Reformer

We shall confine ourselves here to the definition of reformer as one who breaks from the religious tradition in order to restore original truth or ideal in its purer form. The reformer would be closely akin to the founder were it not for the fact that the reformer's efforts are directed at reinterpreting existing tradition. The reformer always finds himself standing at the philosophical crossroads of tradition and innovation. It is important to note that without exception, a reformer is one who understands the tradition thoroughly but realizes that it is wanting.

In summary, these four types of religious personalities we have briefly examined characterize almost every major religion. Given the role these personalities play, it should be fair to argue that religion is not just another organization because, unlike this, religion has a Divine Component, which is probably the hub on which the entire wheel turns.

True Religion and Related Characteristics

Religion and Truth

Since all religions claim that they represent the truth, is it possible that they indeed all teach the same truth in different languages, symbols, ethical codes and theology? Differently put, is there truth in *all religions*? Is it conceivable that only some religions teach the truth but the rest do not? Is it possible that only one religion teaches the truth? Is there *any* truth in religion? Can we arrive at objective answers? At this point one does not expect a member of any religion to answer in the negative. It is logical and reasonable to expect any adherent to argue that there is truth in his or her religion.

In order to address the question of "truth" in religions, we must first turn to founding figures like the Buddha, Christ and Mohammed. These founders believed that there is truth - universal truth that *saves* - in their doctrines. The surprising thing is that some members of these religions argue that only their religion teaches exclusive, ultimate truth. Many theologians, speaking from inside or outside any given religion, articulate truth that is evident and common in several, though not all, religions of the world. What theologians say at least helps us to answer some of the questions as to whether or not there is any truth in world religions. One can say, based on what the scientific religionists have said, that religion does teach not only morality, but truth as well.

While Christian theologians do not all embrace the claim that Christianity is the only religion (based on the gospels) which teaches truth, they concur on the thinking that religion is one means by which eternal truth; i.e., revealed truth, can be made known to humanity. Religions like Islam teach that God has made truth known to humanity; Christianity also argues that God has revealed Divine Truth through human agents to human beings; Judaism believes that God, through Moses, has revealed truth to humanity. It can, therefore, be concluded that there is truth in more than one religion *AND* that *truth* is salvific and liberating. Taking this to its logical conclusion, it can be surmised that this *truth* is in fact the same, expressed in different perspectives by various traditions.

In this book, therefore, scientists who take the position that "all religions are false" must be classified as uninformed in religious methodologies. Consequently, they are not competent to make the right decision or judgment regarding things spiritual.

Since scientists generally make a statement after "testing" theories and hypotheses, any statement a scientist makes without prior "scientific tests" cannot be accepted as true. Similarly, theologians can only claim a truth after they have followed any one of their theological methodologies, including the criterion of coherence and consistence. Stereotypical utterances cannot be used in this book as part of logical progression.

While we cannot embrace a blanket statement by some scholars who argue that "there is truth and saving power in all religions," we are persuaded to endorse the claim by people like Ghandi that, "(1) all religions are true and (2) all religions have some error in them." Our stance here is influenced by our study of chief characteristics of religions worthy of the name. Another thinker, Ramakrishna, makes a statement worth noting in this context: "Different creeds are but different paths to reach the Almighty. . . . Every religion is nothing but one of such paths that lead to God" (*Wadsworth Publishing 1999, 30*).

There may be value in the Hindu position that "each of the orthodox schools of Hindu philosophy is true up to a point and that no single school is the exclusive custodian of truth" (*Ibid*). Overall, there are certain characteristics of major religions, which we should examine here.

Chief Characteristics of Major Religions

It has been our observation that all religions - at least major religions of the world - have the following characteristics:

1. Religion has some beliefs in either a deity, a God a higher principle, or an ideal. This may be expressed in various ways, but there exists the object of worship without which a movement cannot quite qualify as a religion.
2. Religion has some doctrine on the path, salvation, or eternal life, or immortality of the soul, or morality. Whether the religion is exclusive or inclusive, all the same, it teaches some doctrine believed to have been given by the object of worship of that particular religion.
3. Religion has a code of conduct/morality. It teaches the followers to live a certain type of lifestyle. Morality includes codes of conduct and principles concerning right and wrong.
4. Religion has myths. These are stories about truth, life, or

theological concepts. Myths serve a very important function in that they create a vehicle through which doctrine is explained to the adherents. All religions include mythic conceptions. Myths concern what lies beyond the reaches of historical inquiry.

5. Religion has sacred literature - whether it is oral or written - it does not matter. What is important is the fact that there is a vehicle through which the teachings are conveyed generation after generation. Some religions only commit to written form of literature after a long period of "keeping together" a collection of sacred literature. Note that before the age of the printing press, many communities relied on oral transmission.

6. Religion must have a set of rituals and/or ceremonies which express not only the beliefs but also theological concepts. Rituals are ways of "acting out" or "putting to action" words and concepts of one's religion. Differently put, rituals are the quintessential religious acts; a means of sanctification i.e., putting things into their proper places. Rituals are acted out in response to a wide range of human concerns.

7. Religion has some form of revelation. Revelation is religion's way of knowing that which the mind/reason cannot otherwise conceive. Revelation is knowledge given through human reason - or in spite of it. Generally, revelation is conceived of as external knowledge fused into the mind of a particular individual. In strict theological terms, revelation is regarded as superior to mere reason. Thus, revelation could be conceived as Divinely-Inspired knowledge. Even in the case of non-theistic religions like Buddhism, revelation plays a central role.

8. Religion has some form of mystery. As a spiritual phenomenon, mystery is that happening which words cannot explain but the mind grasps the facts and effects of such a mystery. People who belong to so-called "advanced religions" tend to minimize the aspect of "mystery" in their theological vocabulary and thought process, yet they entertain revelation. They do not seem to realize that these two concepts are two sides of the same coin! Revelation is the "breaking open" of the mystery.

9. Religion has some concept of a system of evil, which may even be personified.

Of course, these characteristics can be found in some cults that do not qualify to be called religions. Furthermore, if someone wished to fake a religion, they would want to make sure that most of these characteristics were included in order for their efforts to succeed. What no one can succeed in fabricating is the revelation, because it is an independent occurrence. God cannot be fabricated. Put differently, revelation cannot be caused to happen by any human being, no matter how ambitious one may be.

Finally, in this author's opinion, the "God element" is the Ultimate characteristic of a true religion. If there is no God-component, what we have is a case of sociological phenomenon disguised as religion.

Does God Exist?

We have defined religion as primarily "belief in God or gods..." It is therefore fitting that we discuss whether or not such an entity called God (god) does in fact exist. Is there some truth in the atheist position that religion and God is a figment of human imagination? Discourse regarding the existence of God is one of the most stimulating intellectual topics in academia. Questions and curiosity have ranged from whether there exists an infinite, absolute *BEING*, defined by Anselm as "that than which nothing greater can be conceived;" whether such a *BEING* is the embodiment of the Ultimate God; whether such is the essence of the whole concept of love, and so forth; to whether this God is eternal, moral and perfect. The test of belief rests on this concept of the Living God who exists, has always existed and will always be.

For others, the real question is: if there is a God who is good, loving, almighty and all-knowing, how does one reconcile such existence with the rampant presence of evil in the world? Are there two political kingdoms: God's and Satan's? If "God is God" (according to G. Muzorewa's definition), why does God permit all the suffering, pain, catastrophes, disease, evil and misfortunes that cause much anguish to so many of "God's children"?

There is a school of thought among Christians that says God allows "God's children" to suffer so that they may develop character. Within the same school of thought, the conviction is that God actually causes people to suffer in order to test their faith. These people refer to Job and Abraham in the Bible and say that is how our mighty, loving God tests us. Most serious theologians no longer accept this theology also. The reader is invited to reflect seriously on this theology. Studies on theodicy have been done already with results indicating that our knowledge of God continues to unfold. Consequently, "we will understand it all bye-and-bye!"

Here we shall simply discuss a few of the several traditional arguments for the existence of God. A Student of religion or philosophy may seek to study all the classical arguments in order to explore various approaches to the subject. Let us begin with the cosmological argument. This and the rest of the arguments simply "infer" the existence of God without giving the reader "test tube type" of evidence becauses of the nature of the subject.

a. *The Cosmological Argument*

The cosmological argument is based on observations about the Universe. The assumption is that after observing certain facts about the universe, it is reasonable to infer that God exists. Also, another assumption is that all observable phenomena must have a cause and it is this cause that we think of as God - referred to by some philosophers of religion as "The Uncaused Cause," or "The First Mover."

Let us think for a moment of an eagle in flight. One infers that for this motion to occur, there must be a cause for it. The shape of the bird and the atmosphere all have something to do with "flight." Or, consider a seed which, upon interacting with certain necessary conditions for its gemination, will grow into a huge oak tree, for instance. Furthermore, we observe that in this Universe, things come into existence and they also cease to exist. For instance human beings are born and will die: what are we to infer?

The cosmological argument contends that only an unlimited, self-existent *BEING* can account for the Universe. In order to explain activities such as motion, growth, death, and the like, we have to infer the existence of a necessary *BEING* which is Eternal, First Mover and Uncaused Cause. Things just do not happen without a cause or a reason.

According to St. Thomas Aquinas, things move either when they are acted upon by another, or by themselves provided that they have a soul. Even things that move by themselves do of necessity move because something else has caused them to. But such movement is not indefinite. It can be traced to where it begins to avoid an infinite regress or endless series of subsequent movers. Thomas argues that this "endlessness" comes to a final halt when it gets to this Unmoved Mover, God. Thus, God is the First Mover, the initial and underlying cause of all things in the universe - great or small. We also observe with Thomas that some things are produced by others. Nothing is able to be a sufficient cause in itself. There must be a First Efficient Cause which itself is not caused - rather it is the Cause of causality. This Cause is what we call God.

Thomas further argued that all finite entities come into existence and cease to exist. Because everything is contingent, it can be inferred that there must have been a time when nothing existed which now exists only because some pre-existent *BEING* caused it to come into being. The basic argument is that: for there to be anything at all, there must have always been something rather than nothing. It is this "something" which is necessarily eternal and is what is called God, the UnCaused Cause, the First Mover of all contigent things.

Another way to argue for the existence of God who is perfect and eternal comes from conceiving "a perfect being." According to Rene Descartes, a human being who is imperfect and finite can only conceive of "a perfect being" because such a being exists outside of a human being. Otherwise the idea of "a perfect being" could not have originated from an imperfect and finite being. For Descartes, the idea of God is not derived through the human senses. Neither is it a construct of humanity's finite intellect. The only way a finite being can process the idea of perfection is if the perfect itself caused the imperfect to process such an idea. Put differently, it is argued that God has stamped the idea of the Divine in humanity's faculties. Furthermore, the implication of this trend of thought is that humanity is actually capable of not only conceptualizing but also knowing that God exists.

Some philosophers added this idea of God by inferring that this eternal necessity which caused everything to be could not itself be a product of what is finite. Rather, the finite must have been made to come into being by the infinite, the eternal, the First Cause, known as God.

b. *The Ontological Argument*

St. Anselm, a distinguished theologian and Archbishop of Canterbury initially formulated the ontological argument which attempts to demonstrate that logically, God's existence cannot be denied by any rational mind. The ontological argument is actually a formal proof of the existence of God. In his own work, *The Proslogium*, Anselm states his commitment: "I set to seek within myself whether I might discover one argument which needed nothing else than itself alone for its proof; and which by itself might suffice to show that God truly exists" (*Anselm 1926, 1*). Anslem went beyond the idea of "just an idea" to an idea/concept of and experience as reality. For him it is one thing for an idea of something to exist in the mind and quite another for the referent of such an idea to exist in the reality. For example, Santa Claus exists only as an idea but not as an objective reality. For Anselm, the idea of Perfect Being, the idea of "that than which nothing greater can be conceived" cannot just exist in the mind alone. Perfection, for Anselm, cannot be just conceptual divorced from reality. In fact, God is such a perfect being. God exists in the mind as well as objective reality. This makes God's existence uniquely necessary. Anselm argues that God cannot be conceived not to exist. Anything which is contingent being can be conceived as not existing at some point, but not so with God. God cannot be conceived as not having been in existence because God is eternal. Time, by which we measure periods and eons, is part of what God has brought into being. Therefore, God cannot be less than what God has created. So, God necessarily exists "more truly than all other things and hence in a higher degree than all others" (*Anselm Proslogium, 1926, 8-9*). Anselm makes the assertion that God necessarily exists and cannot logically be conceived not to exist. Other philosophers have also concurred with Anselm on the contention that "existence is implicit in the idea of God." Contingent nonexistence cannot apply to God. A perfect being cannot lack existence or else it would not be perfect. God necessarily possesses every sort of perfection. Logically speaking, God's essence and God's existence are one and the same. Therefore, it is inferred that the Being who is perfect and exists is the same we call God.

c. *The Teleological Argument*

Perhaps the most appealing argument for the existence of God is the teleological argument also known as "the argument from design." This argument is based on what most human beings perceive as a pattern in the universe. Is orderliness of the Universe by sheer chance or is it by design? Is it by "random evolutionary process" or is there an intelligent purpose? These are interesting and persuasive questions which have drawn the attention of theologians as well as philosophers, scientists as well as ordinary people.

Teleological argument maintains that it is more reasonable to assume that it reflects the aims of Divine Intelligence. Numerous hardcore scientists agree with the physicist Stephen Hawking that "the odds against a universe like ours coming out of something like the Big Bang are enormous" (*Boslough, Stephen Hawking's Universe, 121*).

That nature is remarkably orderly and systematic is self-evident. Though with imperfections, the human society (like the universe) shows some design. For instance, the male is equipped sexually to enter the female; the female is physiologically designed to give birth and so on. There is harmony among the stars, the earth and the oceans. Indeed wherever there is order in human experience, we find a mind at work, planning, designing and intending. The anatomy of every species of animal is a prodigious display of proportion, intricacy and adaption.

The teleological argument maintains that the order reflected in nature is best accounted for by attributing it to intelligent design. A Christian theologian and philosopher, William Paley, has argued that if one was to find a watch in the forest, one would most likely infer that someone had "designed" such an item. So is the case with the Universe. A careful analysis of any aspect of the Universe leads the observer to infer that there must be a big mind - a *mastermind*. That mastermind is God.

Chapter 2

African Traditional Religion

On the continent of Africa, there are three major faiths which are counted among the world's major religions, namely: Christianity, Islam and African traditional religion, which is also one of the world's oldest religions. To indicate when this religion might have originated an expert on African studies, Geoffrey Parrinder, is among a few that give us a clue. He says, "the religions of Africa fall into three natural groups: traditional religions, Christianity and Islam, in order of appearance" (Parrinder 1969, 8). We may also add depth and dimension to Parrinder's statement by inferring that since conclusive evidence of the first human being was found on the continent, God has made Godself known to such a community from time immemorial. Further, since there was no natural boundary between what is now Arabia, where the Garden of Eden is traditionally located, and the continent, we further infer that when God walked in the "cool of the day," that was on the continent where God first revealed Godself. However, our task here is not to argue dates or origin of African religion. Rather, we simply discuss African religion as the world's oldest major religion, which western scholars have for the longest time, pretended did not exist. If it does, it has been relegated to the periphery as one of the Primal Religions. This ethnocentric attitude toward anything African is common and typical among many westerners. Yet it is, of course, very wrong. Afrocentric studies indicate that Africa is the origin of world civilizations. For example, Prof. Molefi Asante of Temple University argues that any study of world civilization ought to begin with Africa - i.e., Nubia, Egypt, etc.

African traditional religion does not have a single, individual founder as is the case with the other two. It is community religion which was the response to God's revelation because God - the creator of humanity - is the object of its worship. African religion believes that all creation is the work of the Supreme Spiritual Being known by many names, most of which mean: The Creator. (see appendix G.) Therefore, to describe this religion, the natural starting point is the relationship between the Creator, God, and the first human community to know and worship God - the African Traditionalist. Before the concept of religion was made complicated by the 19th and 20th Century scholars like Herbert L. Spencer, Karl Marx, Edward B. Taylor, F. Max Muller, religion was simply defined as the awareness, reverence, worship and a feeling of dependence upon the Creator.

For the first Africans, worshiping God was not viewed as returning a favor to God "who came to the world to die for our sins" (Christianity). Neither was religion conceived of as "humanity's total trusting surrender to Allah" (Islam), or "maintenance of a covenant between humanity and God" (Judaism). Rather, religion was simply this "spiritual consciousness of a sense of dependence;" being aware that humanity ought to give praise, acknowledge and revere the author of all creation - one whose origin is unthinkable, existence is unquestionable and immutable, power is ultimate, caring is at best taken for granted and at worst mentioned in passing! Religion was spontaneous, learned and residual from generation to generation, but not proselytized.

It is no wonder African religion has no particular individual founder. The community spontaneously felt the Numinous, the Awesome, the Ultimate, the Almightiness, the Supremeness of the Creator. Unlike religions founded by particular individuals who "saw" something or "felt" something, or were "commanded" something by God, African religion happens every time, everywhere, to everyone (hence, there is no need to proselytize). Put differently, African religion is a way of life, rather than a momentary event or occasion that is repeated in life only at certain times.

Again, the 19th and 20th Century scholars did not recognize African religion as one because it was "a way of life," versus an event at a specific time on a particular day. For those accustomed to organizing major religions by "preaching and teaching," passing religions - do's and don'ts - African religion threw them off because, rather than being organized, it organizes the people into a community; rather than giving people the Divine Law to live by, it causes the adherents to devise ways or codes of conduct to observe in compliance with Divine nature with which the community is in relation. Put differently, African religion provides a wholistic atmosphere. It is a way of life rather than a thing to obey. Foreign missionaries ignored it because they assumed it was all culture and no religion. That is how African religion is intertwined with everyday life.

For this reason, African religion traditionally does not have "a written text" which would be accessible only to the learned anyhow. Rather, the text is written on every individual's heart. The rationale for this is, for a person to be alive, she or he must have a heart, and if one has this, one naturally has the sacred text! As the heart is the essence of human existence, so is God about whom the heart "speaks." God is the center. By the way, it is a distortion of truth to say religion is the center of African morality. God is. Religion is a description of human behavior in response to our relationship, response, awareness, praise of God who is at the center of it all.

Various cosmogonic myths folk tales indicate that God (the Creator) holds a central position in traditional life. There is no traditional theological belief apart from belief in the Creator. All morality focuses on this sense, this "feeling of dependence, gratitude and belonging." Most taboos in African life are intended to manifest as well as protect our awareness of the Supreme Being - God. Not only is God the Creator, but is also one who conceived and organized the universe, including creatures, deities and inanimate objects. Adherents attribute the creator with providence, omnipotence, transcendence, immanence and eternity as well as aseity. According to some sources, God is distinguished from all other beings on the basis that "every other being is created - God pre-existed the world and everything else that is known to exist" (Metuah 1981, 33).

Further, the language of African belief in God makes it clear that there can only be **one** God - the Creator. "For the Igbo, Chukwu is one and can only be one. Chukwu Abo, two Gods, or Chukwu Ga, many Gods cannot be imagined" (Metuah 1981, 35). Any African community's concept of God conveys this Divine Unity. Professor John Mbiti writes, "by attributing omniscience to God, African peoples are placing Him (sic) in the highest possible position" (Mbiti 1970, 3). Mbiti also says, "In these names and short phrases, God is described as one to whom complete wisdom, knowledge or understanding belongs" (Mbiti 1970, 3).

God is believed to be self-existent - aseity. Various traditional communities express the belief that "God has always been, is immortal, and upholds the universe" (Mbiti op cit). My own people, the Shona of Zimbabwe, believe that God is *Mu-wanikwa, Chidzachepo, Mu-tangakurgara* - all of which describe God as the original, the Uncaused

Cause, the one who was in the eternal beginning, has always been and will be forever respectively. Note that, philosophically and etymologically, the Shona prefixes "Mu" and "Chi" designate unicity (absolutely one). Since most Africans tend to name only what they have experienced (or seen), it is credible to argue conclusively that, based on what and whom God has revealed to the Africans, and on the basis of the etymological evidence, African religion is the first monotheism. Further, philosophically speaking, if God is "the Creator," God, *ipso facto*, is one. Monist philosophers have argued this view in a very persuasive and convincing logic.

As one race that acknowledges one creator, Africans worship one God. Hence it is more proper to speak of "African Religion," rather than African religions in the plural. Since religion designates "a relationship," there is only one such relationship (one people of African descent, worshiping one God, their Creator)! We suspect that the mistake of talking of "African religions" in the plural originated from eurocentric chauvinism that assumed that Africans worshiped **many** gods, after all in their numerous languages, their names for God vary. However, just because there are numerous African names for the creator does not necessarily mean that there are many creators. This is fairly fundamental. In fact, on a positive note, the fact that the same God is named by various regions in their native languages clearly indicates indigenous familiarity with the creator (see appendix G). Mbiti is correct to argue that because God is *Spirit*, it is clear that such spirit is one and omnipresent. In addition, we agree with Mbiti that "God is the parent and people are his (sic) children. In some places he (sic) is even called the Great Ancestor, The Elder, The Grandfather, meaning that it is from him (sic) that all people and all things originated" (Mbiti 1975, 47).

Thus, the God of African traditional religion is viewed as the Ultimate, the Supreme, the Highest, the First, One who is like no other, One who was not created, One who created the universe. Since all these adjectives and superlatives describe God, what is the African concept of God? After a brief discussion on the hierarchy of being we will have to focus on "God."

The Hierarchy of Beings in African Cosmology

The Spirit-World is hierarchical according to kind and importance:

1. The Creator ranks highest and wields the most power;
2. The Deities who are generally at the disposal of both God and the living;
3. The spirit forces;
4. The ancestors who actively involve themselves in the affairs of their respective families;
5. The physical or material world is the least powerful and most transient. It is wholly at the mercy of the spirit entities.

Now, let us discuss these in some detail, bearing in mind that although we talk in terms of "hierarchy," everything belongs together. African spirituality is wholistic.

1. The Creator transcends everything which is the work of the Creator's own making. The deities are messengers and representatives in nature. However they do not reside "in place of" the Creator. The Creator is transcendent, all pervasive, omnipresent and omniscient. The deities merely serve as manifestations of the Great Spirit God who is in and through every creature. There is a divine inter connectedness throughout creation in heaven and on earth.
2. The deities, best described by the Ibgo, for example, as Mmuo, rank second in African cosmology. The non-human spirits serve as the agents of the Creator. Some deities live near God while others live on earth. Their primary responsibility is service to humanity such as: fertility, air, morality, good fortune, protection, healing and so forth. All of this means that African religious beliefs do not leave anything to accident. There is a power responsible - a cause - for every happening. Furthermore, there is a purpose for everything.
3. The Arusi (spirit forces) are different from the deities in that they sometimes act "irrationally" whereas the deities are always rational since they represent God - the source or origin of reason and wisdom. The Arusi can actually be instructed by human beings to cause vengeance on an adversary. Worse yet, they may be "owned" by a clan, family, or even an individual who may choose to manipulate them.
4. The Ndi Mmuo (the disembodied spirits) are the spirits of the dead. The Ndichie, meaning ancestors, are the spirits of good people who have reached their proper destination - the spiritual abode. Immoral spirits wander between the spiritual abode and the physical world. These are the evil spirits, witches, etc.
5. The Uwa (the visible world) consists of human beings,

ranging from the newborn child to the aged. Among the African people all human beings are recognized as such. There is even a "proverb" which says: "Even a poor person is a human being." This means the worth of human life is not dependent on materialism.

In traditional religion, Africans affirm life - large families, prosperity, and numerous relatives - all signify blessedness. Therefore, religion for the traditionalist is constant contact with God, the Creator of everything, including the material and the immaterial, the spiritual and supernatural beings. Africans have been appropriately described as notoriously religious because all aspects of life are spiritually driven. The ulterior motive for all behavior is to do what is right, not what is wrong. Wrongness is destructive, rightness affirms life. Rightness is the path to external living.

The Concept of God

The idea of God, the most important component in African traditional religion, exerts a primary influence on African thinking. Most scholars agree that all African peoples believe in one God. For instance, Professor Gabriel M. Setiloane states that to note this attribute among Sotho-Tswana peoples is to state the obvious (1976b, 79). Other theologians have emphasized the fact that Africans have always believed in the one God. Further, Professor Idowu says: "There is no place, age, or generation which did not receive at some point in its history some form of revelation" (1975, 140).

Idowu finds that although God is one, various communities may have different names for God. The many names of God, however, need not imply polytheistic practices in African religion; it is the same God whose self-revelation occurs throughout the world. My interpretation is supported by other scholars even informed expatriates who say:

> the God of African traditional religion and Christianity is in fact the same. God who revealed himself fully in Jesus Christ is none other than the one who has continually made himself known to African religious experience (1974a, 81].

The revelation to which both Idowu and McVeigh refer is one of the bases on which African traditionalists claim to know God. Consequently, Setiloane says:

> The Sotho-Tswana God, according to me, the Ngo peoples' God, according to Gaba, and the Kikuyu peoples' God, according to Kibicho, could never die, because *It* has no human limitations and *It* is so immense, incomprehensible, wide, tremendous, and unique [1979].

This assertion not only reinforces the African belief that there is only one God, but also demonstrates that the categories of male and female do not apply to God. Setiloane uses "It" for lack of a better "translation" to express the being of God beyond gender language.

The African belief in the one God whose self-revelation is continuous leads us to the concept of natural theology. The use of both general and special revelation enables African theologians, as Dr. Harry Sawyerr has remarked, to present God as both immanent and transcendent (1963), a concept that underscores the importance of traditional religion in the formulation of cosmology.

One of the most important tasks of African religious thinking is to be able to articulate God's relationship to humanity. In this regard the traditional belief that God is both transcendent and immanent (1970a, 41) provides a framswork for understanding how the African views God. African theology has developed this concept in such a way that the African experience of God's presence and seeming "absence" affirm God's omnipresence. Gabriel Setiloane maintains that "God is everywhere, involved in everything...although *It* is in some way located in the sky and in the bowels of the earth...yet *It* controls everything" (1976b, 82.)

These concepts of God make African believers feel a natural closeness to the one God, the only Supreme Being known in African traditional religion. God is not regarded as a thing but personality with qualities that exceed gender categories.

African scholars share the view that God is the *Original Source* and the *Beginning* of all things (1970, 21). In Idowu's words, "Only Deity is the absolute origin of all things, only he has absolute power and authority" (1975, 160). John Mbiti has said: "Strictly, speaking, Theology has to do primarily with God, and all other things must spring from that" (1972b, 186). For instance, justice originates with God.

This is another attribute of God that is important for an African spirituality. Setiloane declares that God preserves justice (1976b, 83). Other African theologians recognize that there is a point beyond which human and spiritual powers cannot go and only God will remain ultimately responsible. In traditional life, God is believed to intervene on certain occasions for the purpose of preserving justice. In its search for principles of justice, an African theology draws from African traditional legal procedures. African scholars are establishing a theological concept of justice such that when they address political matters their theological decisions are grounded in genuinely African tenets. God the creator, is just.

Africans believe that while God is invisible, God's acts are tangible. Herein lies a potential doctrine of pneumatology. A traditional understanding of the concept of God as Spirit is common in African traditional religion. Setiloane says: "It [God] manifests *Itself* in physical phenomena, such as lightning and thunder" (1976b, 80). This is why Africans believe both that God is spirit and that God's presence can be felt and experienced physically. Religion among Africans is a way of everyday realities as already noted.

The commonest African concept of God is that God is the Creator. As Mbiti points out:

> Practically all African people consider God as Creator, making this the commonest attribute of the works or activities of God. The concept is expressed through saying directly that God created all things, through giving him the name of Creator (or its equivalent), and through addressing him in prayer as the Creator or Maker [1970b, 45].

On this concept, every African thinker has something positive to say. Sawyerr's *God: Ancestor or Creator?* deals directly with this particular belief. The creation myths in the traditional worldview portray God as the Creator or Maker. With this concept African scholars must begin and end their task of theologizing.

Although there are numerous other African concepts of God, it is not necessary to discuss each one because our purpose is not to catalogue the many African ideas of God. Our concern is to show the importance of African traditional religion. However, there can be no adequate discussion of African religion without an examination on the ancestral spirits.

The Concept of Ancestry

The concept of ancestral spirits, a major ingredient in African traditional religion, plays a major part in African spirituality.

Harry Sawyerr describes the traditional African sense of the presence of the dead: "It is this fact of presence that has led to the belief in the continued existence of the ancestral spirits and in their influence on their descendants" (1968, 60). C. G. Baeta makes a similar observation

(1968, 60). This presence of the ancestral spirits or their equivalent in any given community augments the African spiritual understanding of the community.

Ancestors occupy a significant place in traditional religion because they are believed to possess supernatural powers. Sawyerr observes that "the presence of the dead is assumed and invoked when the life of the tribe is threatened with disaster" (1968, 26). For Idowu, "Many ancestors remain...spiritual superintendents of family affairs and continue to bear their titles of relationship like 'father' or 'mother" (Idowu 1975, 184). African thinkers draw significant insights from the belief in ancestral spirits. The importance of this belief for traditional religion also lies in the fact that ancestrology properly places emphasis on the reality of the spirit world. Africans believe that the ancestors provide a link with the life-giving spirit world because ancestors are an inseparable part of our everyday life with all its material aspects.

It is almost universally held by African religious philosophers that their people believe that the spiritual is just as important and consequential as the physical. "Hence, a living human being can carry on a conversation with the spiritual or invisible living-dead" (Mbiti 1970a, 11). That African traditional religion does not simply consist in the everyday physical realities but also involves spiritual realities is best dramatized in the prominent place given to the ancestors in worship and thought. This fact makes African traditional religion a live background for African spirituality.

Geoffrey Parrinder refers to this influence when he says that "all Ibgo believe that their lives are profoundly influenced by their ancestors, and this belief has far-reaching sociological consequences" (1974, 57). A vital role of ancestors in African traditional religion is to hold the community together through moral code of which the ancestors are guardians. Where ancestors are venerated, they are "factors of cohesion in African society" (Idowu 1975, 185). Many Africans contend that "the ancestors are the custodians of the morality of the tribe or community: hence ethical conduct is determined by reference to the ancestors' (Fashole-Luke 1974, 213). M. J. McVeigh writes:

> African attention is centered on the ancestors who are looked up to as the guardians of individuals, families, and the community as a whole. Those in flesh constantly seek communion with the departed [1974a, 103].

Life is inconceivable without this interdependence between the living and the living-dead. In the same vein, Professor John Pobee discusses the role of the ancestors as godly: "God the Supreme Being has delegated authority to the *abosom* (gods) and to the *mpanyinto* (the ancestors), who, therefore, act *in loco Dei* and *pro Dei*" (1979, 46). This is why, due to a lack of understanding, missionaries assumed that Africans worship their ancestors.

A significant point that needs to be highlighted is the cleansing process which the would-be ancestor goes through prior to installation. In this process (*Chenura*) the community forgives the would-be ancestor of all sin committed even inadvertently. That ritual entitles the now "ancestor" to commune with the saints gone on before as well as to communicate with God at a spiritual level. Thus, when Africans talk of the ancestors as righteous and just, they also imply that ancestors are creatures that do not do any wrong and consequently are able to regulate morality with authority in the community.

Regarding the doctrine of sin, the people and God can work together in their respective capacities to cleanse, forgive, and therefore save the fallible human being. The ancestor then becomes a saint, charged by God with the responsibility of ensuring the welfare of the people of his or her own tribe.

In traditional religion, the ancestors are believed to watch over their own folk. They seek to please and preserve their living relatives, provided that the latter pledge to appease their ancestors. The relationship is mutual and generally limited to the clan in question. This exclusive tendency of Africans is not necessarily a condemnation of other races. It is merely an attempt to affirm their own culture. I believe that God chooses the agents, in this case the ancestors, who relate to a particular people and works through those agents to save the people. It is in this sense that Pobee says: "There is a dependence of the living on the ancestors whose authority is nevertheless derived from God." Since the ancestors have been endowed with the power to enable African survival, Pobee concludes that "the attitude of the living toward the ancestors is something more than veneration" (1979, 47).

The ancestral concepts establish a connection among the individual, the community, and God. In the other direction, too, God channels forgiveness through the community to the individual. Setiloane correctly explains how this phenomenon actually unfolds:

> A young man, wishing to make an approach to *MODIMO* [God], approaches his elder brother, who approaches his father, who approaches his grandfather...and the request is passed up the hierarchy of *badimo* until it reaches one sufficiently senior to address *MODIMO*

directly [1976b, 65].

We can infer that the ancestors play a vital role in African knowledge of God because they are spiritual. Therefore, African religion and other revealed religions tend to be compartible.

Such hedonism should enhance it. This integration is important for African theology because it leaves no possibility of a negative syncretism.

African theology and ancestrology try to interpret historical events, such as a series of deaths in one family. However it is believed that the power to understand such events emanates from God. The ancestors are merely God's agents and creations. In fact, Africans who is also the ultimate source of comfort in times of grief believe that their ancestors have the power to control and regulate cosmological cause and effect. Consequently, traditional religion upholds the belief that ancestors, if well-pleased, can make things go well for their living families. By the same token, if they are displeased, the ancestors may invoke punitive action on their families. Good and evil have profound ramifications among the Africans and are taken very seriously in traditional religion.

The Concepts of Good and Evil

Concepts of good and evil constitute a major part of traditional religion. An African decalogue (oral) that regulates their people developed ethics separate from theology. The importance of good and evil in traditional religion makes it a vital source for knowledge of God. The Law is written on their heart.

There are African creation myths like the biblical story of Eden that say that God created humanity and put the first group of people in paradise (Mbiti 1970b, 166). Everything was good in the beginning. In fact, some African tribes believe that "the first people lived happily, lacking nothing, as God provided them with food, shelter, and immortality" (Mbiti 1970b, 167). So when Africans do everything possible to avoid evil, or when they deal with it, they are seeking to capture that original state. Unlike western philosophy, which spend much time trying to establish the origin of evil, traditional religion invests much time dealing with the causes and effects of evil (Pobee 1979, 99). Because African religion has this background, it takes the form of a problem-solving religion, rather than a problem-oriented one.

Most African theologians who treat the subject of evil and good in an African cosmology agree that there is evil in this world. Evil is a reality, though it is not clear where it originates. Parrinder argues that some scholars believe that evil may be attributed to the ancestors (1974, 60). There are some African theologians, however, who differ with Parrinder, believing that evil has other human, spiritual, or natural forces as its agents. They make the point clear that the agent itself is basically not evil; it becomes evil insofar as it causes evil to happen. This view is consistent with the Bible, which teaches that everything that was created by God is therefore good. African religion conveys a doctrine of humanity that affirms the goodness of human nature. The doctrine of original sin is unknown because creation is all good.

That traditional religion has rituals that can control or cope effectively with evil when it occurs makes ritual important for African spirituality.

Sacrifice is one example, treated thoroughly by Harry Sawyerr (Dickson and Ellingworth 1971, 57). Traditional rituals bring useful theological insights to the knowledge of God, cosmology and evil.

Pobee classifies evil according to its causes: the primary cause and the secondary cause (1979, 100). Witches are the first category, while any other human being who does wrong belongs to the second category. The difference is that witches are possessed with evil involuntarily, while others decide to indulge in an evil act. Many African theologians would agree with Pobee's view that "there is at one point or other, human responsibility or input into the occurrence of evil" (Pobee 1979, 100). This does not, however, make African humanity inherently evil. Even a witch is not evil by nature since, as a human being, she is good; she is evil insofar as the spirit of evil possess her (Pobee 1979, 100). Thus in the African context, witchcraft is a practical, tangible example of evil that possesses a human being who is otherwise good. An African doctrine of humanity that is formulated in the light of this distinction between evil by nature and evil by possession addresses the question of the problem of evil in a fresh manner.

Since the basic agents of evil are human persons, what, then is the African concept of humanity? This classical question has occupied most African theologians, social scientists and other scholars. To comprehend this concept, first it is important to understand the meaning and role of mythology.

Mythology and Morality in African Religion

Humanity is "being in relation." The traditional African is defined by his or her family (and there is no such thing as "extended family"!), clan, tribe and community. Being is shaped and informed by relationships - physical, spacial and spiritual interrelatedness. Relationships also extend in time. The meaning and origin of these relationships is communicated as well as passed on from generation to generation through a variety of means, for instance, myths.

Mythology is intended to explain and justify the network of relationships which does not only connect human beings but these to the entire universe of which Africans feel they are a part. A look at a typical myth, for example, gives us a clue of how humanity is interconnected and linked up with the entire universe. One of the major functions of morality is to maintain such interconnectedness.

Myth

Myth is simply defined as "story." The word myth itself is of Greek origin: Mythoi which means stories. It is mainly Christians who, at the inception of their religion, gave the term "Mythoi" the connotation of "false stories" because they wanted to discredit Greek "stories of the gods and about the gods." From that era on, "myth" has been associated with "unfounded stories." It is not surprising that to date people talk of "telling stories" to man a bunch of lies! Yet, in its original sense "mythoi" or myth as we say in English, simply means "a story," and generally a story is a narration of what happened. Granted the meanings of words change over a period of time. Here, we define the term myth thus, a story of sacred or holy significance. Whether the story is true or false is another matter. Typically, however, such stories are told to fulfil a particular function. So, it is not so much about historicity or ahistoricity as it is about explaining truths. Let us take a quick look at some myths.

a. Yoruba creation myth. According to the Yoruba people, Oduduwa - coming from somewhere far away - from Arabia, perhaps, brought the Yoruba into their homeland, ruling them from Ile-Ife. He then gave birth to the men and women who were to rule or provide rulers for other Yoruba Communities.

b. The Lugbra creation myth. According to the Lugbra people, God in His transcendent aspect created the first men, husband and wife, a long time ago. These two bore a son and a daughter who mated and produced male and female children.

	Human population began to increase on earth.
c.	<u>The Shilluk creation myth</u> (of humanity). The Shilluk believe that God used clay of different colors in making human beings. This explains why human beings come in different skin pigmentation.
d.	<u>The Bambuti creation myth</u> (of humanity). The Bambuti Pygmies tell the story of humanity's creation this way. God made the body of the first human being by kneading, and then "covered him with a skin and poured blood into his lifeless body." Then the man took his first breath. Then God whispered into his ear these words: You will beget children who will live in the forest.

Such stories are found in most communities. What is amazing is the fact that they all assume that God is the creator of humanity. It is no wonder one of the names for God among the Shona people of Zimbabwe is *Musikavanhu*, transliterated, the creator of humanity.

Almost all myths of creation mention God - one God, who gives instruction to humanity on how to live in a community. Meaningful life is "life in relation," not only with one another but with the Creator as well. For this reason, morality is an important part of African belief system. In fact much of African religiosity hinges on morality as such. Scholars believe that, while it is true that the ancestors are the guardians of morality, God is the ultimate guardian of not only morality but humanity and the entire universe.

The Concept of Humanity in Community

The concept of humanity, which has largely determined all other African cosmological concepts, is central in traditional religion. How African humanity has traditionally perceived itself is of primary importance to religion in general, African traditional religion in particular.

Mbiti summarizes the perspective of most African scholars:

> Since African peoples consider the universe to be centered on man, it is to be expected that there would be more myths about man's own origin and early state than about anything else [1975a, 77].

Since African traditionalist believe that God is where man is and vice versa, it is necessary to highlight the importance of humanity in both African traditional religion and African theology. Elsewhere Mbiti informs us that "it is generally acknowledged that God is the originator of man, even if the exact methods of creating man may differ according to the myths of different peoples" (1970a, 120). Pobee finds it difficult to define African humanity because "*Homo africanus* is a multiheaded hydra" (1979, 18). Yet, difficult though it may be to describe, Africans have a certain concept of humanity that can be articulated.

In his article "The Theological Estimate of Man" (1969) Swailem Sidhom discusses the African view of humanity. Most theologians agree with him that African humanity is defined in the context of the community. "All that goes into the making of man is incorporated in the complex unity of the tribe, outside of which all others are strangers and inferiors, if not enemies" (Sidhom 1969, 99). This means that any outsider is likely to violate tribal folkways and mores, causing chaos and catastrophes in the community. Foreigners are considered enemies because their motives are likely to be alien to the local tribal interest. Moreover, their loyalties are bound to be elsewhere. All these unknowns threaten peace in the community. So we find that African humanity is primarily defined by a sense of belonging, serving one's own fold and kinship. For the African, it is not enough to be a human being unless one shares a sense of community, one can easily turn out to be an enemy.

African theology may derive the criteria for belonging to a community of believers from this traditional concept of humanity in community. Such a definition of the community of believers takes collective survival very seriously. Thus two major concerns of African theology: solidarity and humanization, find clear expression in the context of the community. In the words of Mercy Oduyoye, a leading African scholar:

> Africans recognize life as life-in-community. We can truly know ourselves if we remain true to our community, past and present. The concept of individual success or failure is secondary. The ethnic group, the locality, are crucial in one's estimation of oneself. Our nature as beings-in-relation is a two-way relation: with God and with our fellow human beings [1979, 110-111].

One is defined in one's own social context, namely one's community.

Among my people, the Shona, every piece of property in the community is referred to as *chedu*, a possessive pronoun that means "ours" as opposed to "mine." This applies even to parents. Under normal circumstances, one would never say *Baba wangu* (my father). One is more apt to say *Baba vedu* (our father). Thus, the individual understands himself or herself in the context of the community, or at least the family.

Strains of Western thought which have been influenced by Descartes's "I think, therefore I am" (*cogito ergo sum*) and Albert Camus's "I rebel - therefore we exist" (Camus 1956,, 22) contrast with African concepts of humanity. The concept of humanity in the African context as described by Mbiti places the emphasis elsewhere.

> Whatever happens to the individual happens to the whole group, and whatever happens to the whole group happens to the individual. The individual can only say: "I am, because we are and since we are, therefore I am" [1970a, 141].

This is the key to the understanding of the African view of humanity, and, in Mbiti's words, "a cardinal point in the understanding of the African view of man" (1970a, 143). Thus African culture is the proper context in which African humanity can be fully comprehended.

Humanity and Morality

The idea of God, the most important component in African traditional religion, influences and to a great extent defines African morality although this morality is not intended to be the means to an end rather it is the end. Put differently, African morality, i.e. doing what is right - is not for the purpose of being rewarded at the end of time as other religions teach. We have stated elsewhere in this chapter that African religion is not an attempt to maintain a covenant, for instance. It is, rather, a way of life. So, doing the right deed is the ideal African lifestyle. When this is not achieved or, worse still, if someone commits a wrong deed, not only the individual but also the whole family or community makes every effort to "right the wrong for the sake of the whole community." Traditional Africans cannot see themselves living in the wrong indefinitely. By the way, this explains why *chenura* is mandatory within twelve months after one has died. The community feels that in order to make sure that the individual's life is spiritually **cleansed**, the ritual cleansing is performed. This is the final human attempt and chance to "right every wrong" the deceased might have committed both vertically and horizontally.

African cosmology is spirit-filled - all happenings in the cosmos are peculiar in that everything is God-centered. Not only is all creation the work and wisdom of God, but is sustained by the same. Natural as well as human-caused events are all interconnected spiritually ultimately. Put differently, there is cause and effect throughout African cosmology. On a larger scale, there is a "dialogue" between the Creator and creation. The result of such dialogue is cosmological homogeneity. In this sense, peace does not only refer to the human community but to the total "cosmological community" - God, deities, spirits, ancestors, nature, humanity, as well as all that appears inanimate. Peace - real peace - can only be achieved when there is a state of total harmony. And, for the African, everything is dependent on morality. In fact, the purpose of religion is to not only teach and instil, but also awaken a sense of morality, Africans believe that even longevity is evidence of sound morality. (By the way, some Eastern religions, such as Taoism, also share this belief based on harmony with nature.. For this reason, old age is revered. The wisdom attributed to the elderly is not so much the knowledge to deal with technology or such things, as it is the wisdom that made it possible for the individual to live in harmony with the whole universe.

We have pointed out that in African cosmology, all creation operates in relation - one to another. Therefore, if a person sins (commits a wrong act) against the Great Spirit, the whole community is responsible. Because of this, every person must contribute to and participate actively in the guardianship of morality. However, it is the ancestors (also known as the living-dead) who take the full responsibility seriously since they are the "official guardians of morality." The myth created by non-African westerners that ancestors punish their family members was their erroneous attempt to explain this fact. Yes, ancestors will punish wrong-doing in order to preserve morality, but their major role is to be the guardian of morality. In their pneumatic state, and in light of their spirit-to-spirit relationship with God, the Great Ancestor, they are in the most strategic position to carry out this tremendous responsibility. In the same vein, ancestors make every provision possible to make their respective family names prosper. For them a good name is as good as riches. So, for the sake of their family's prosperity, ancestors strive to help the living to be in harmony with the cosmos. After all, does wealth not come from the sea below, the earth and the atmosphere? Is good health not a form of wealth? Ancestors are in touch with all these sources and are also well-connected. To achieve all this, the ancestors discovered that the secret is morality and consequent harmony with the entire universe. Unity is power, morality is peace and prosperity and this is power.

Finally, just as one person can cause disaster in the community, making the whole community suffer, the whole community can and does bring healing to the sick or sinful person suffering from his or her misdeeds. Thus, the community has the potential to heal or self-destruct.

Its salvation comes from the spirit world, via the ancestors, the ultimate guardians of morality, and also the clue to immorality.

Summary

We have discussed the concept of God in traditional life and have seen how African religious concepts of God are being formulated within the traditional frame. One of the very important features to bear in mind is that most African scholars agree that numerous Africans acknowledge the one God whose self-manifestation occurs in different ways to different individuals and communities. General revelation that may include special revelation provides African theology with a firm, indigenous doctrine of God that is consistent with African beliefs and with the essence of the gospel.

We have ascertained also how belief in the ancestral spirits sheds light on the doctrine of forgiveness as well as on the idea of life-after-death and the communion of saints. Ancestrology provides a useful framework for the construction of an African Christology because it deals with life beyond mere physical existence. We have also seen that ancestrology adds a spiritual dimension to our understanding of humanity and is a factor in making a community cohere. Therefore, an African doctrine of humanity draws heavily on traditional ancestrology.

We have tried to locate the source of evil as the Africans understand it. African theology can formulate theological concepts that relate to the problem of theodicy, a problem that has been of great concern in Christendom. African traditional religion holds that all good come from God and that evil was not created by God. Without an agent, evil has no effect. We have also discussed the importance of the concept of goodness among the Africans. We have seen that evil and good among the Africans are not abstractions but concrete realities.

African traditional religion is important for the development of African theology in these four ways:

1. In reconciling general and special revelation, African theology can develop concepts that combine the particularity and the generality of the presence of God.
2. It gives the believer some light beyond physical existence. Ancestrology illuminates the mystery of life-after-death. In redefining eschatology to mean a spiritual reality in the here-and-now, traditional religion enables African scholars to affirm spiritual beings in the present life, and not just in the

afterlife.
3. It has a relatively healthy approach to, and understanding of, theodicy.
4. It defines humanity in such a way that only humanizing principles must be adopted in African life.

Finally, although African traditional religion and Christianity are not the same, and need not be, they do share major religious concerns such as the knowledge of God, spiritual existence, good-and-evil, and humanity.

Terms, Concepts, and Words

Traditional religion - African peoples' way of life, including work, worship, death, etc.

Polytheistic practices - worship of more than one God.

Self-revelation - God causing God-self to be known.

Cosmology - a worldview.

Pneumatology - study of the Holy Spirit.

Chenura - ritual cleansing where the ancestor is installed.

Badimo - ancestors (Tswana people of South Africa).

Modimo - God (Tswana language for God).

Syncretism - mixing two or more religious beliefs from various religions.

Ancestrology - study of ancestors.

Topics for Research

1. Define and discuss the role of ancestors.

2. Discuss the concept: *chenura*.

3. Discuss factors that make the ideal community.

4. Discuss African cosmology with a focus on the spirit world.

5. Compare the western concept of kinship to the African understanding.

6. Discuss myths of human origin in Africa.

Chapter 3

Hinduism

General Introduction

Religions of India

During the early first millennium B.C.E., two powerful theological concepts developed in Asia in general, but India in particular: the concepts of Karma and reincarnation. Three schools of thought in India adopted this concept of reincarnation, resulting in the development of these religions: Hinduism, Jainism and Sikhism. Later on, Buddhism also appeared. Many scholars agree that this religion could be designated as an off-shoot of Hinduism actually. Basic to these religions is the belief that "all thoughts and deeds influence our future lives, bringing reward or punishment" (Matthews 2000, 81). This is the essence of the Karma concept. There is yet another concept: that of the caste system. The belief holds that one is born "according to one's karma in prior lives." For most Hindus and Jains, caste is a fact of life.

Here we will focus on one of these four great religions that have developed to maturity in India - Hinduism. Our rationale for selecting Hinduism is that this seems to be the most ancient and possibly the origin of the rest of the others.

Hindu Worldview

Hindu's worldview is primarily informed by the Vedas, which

were recorded about 1200 B.C.E. , about 100 years before the Laws of Manu began, 500 years after the completion of the Laws of Manu (Laws of Manu were compiled about 200 B.C.E. to 200 C.E.). We will discuss these in greater detail later. Hindu worldview enjoys (or suffers from) a variety of expression (depending on how one approaches the subject). Here we prefer to think of this transformation as positive. Let us examine a few concepts: a) The Absolute, b) The Universe, c) Humanity, Problems and Solutions, d) Morality, Rituals and Symbols, and e) Immortality.

a. **The Absolute**

Hindu religious worldview may be best described as henotheistic - "a belief that affirms one deity without denying the existence of others." This concept helps the reader to realize the inappropriateness of such everyday labels as monotheism, polytheism or atheism, because it connotes and underscores one superior God in the presence of lesser gods. The Hindu believes that there is more to the universe than meets the eye. Our whole experience is embraced by a reality of which one needs to be aware in order to better understand the universe and humanity in particular. According to this view, there is a source of energy that serves as the ground of all existence and a variety of "ways" to experience this reality.

For fear they might underestimate a god, the Hindu have preferred to include many personalities. In Hinduism, image worship does not pose any threat to their faith. Hindus believe that it is better for the less informed Hindus to worship several images than to not have a sense of the "ground of all existence." Worshiping at least one god (or even an image) is viewed as a strength. After all, a person who has a sense of "adoration," with time, will learn of the ultimate ground of all being as he or she matures spiritually. In Hindu religion, the adherent will one day realize that there is the divine that transcends the image he or she worships. More advanced worshipers understand images as merely symbols of the various powers (including the ground of all being) at work in the universe. A notion of God is worth more than noting.

In this regard, many Hindus prefer a more personal god, such as Krishna, although a few images of Brahman do exist. According to one Hindu philosopher/theologian, Yajna Valkya, Brahman can be worshiped in numerous names, numbering between 3 to 3300, but, ultimately, there is only one God - all the others are but manifestations of powers. Hindu thought, better referred to as Sanatana Dharma - the eternal law -

ultimately teaches that there is one reality which sustains all existence. Consequently, Hinduism has led millions of human beings to understand (gain insight into) "the human condition, the ultimate human goal, and effective ways to attain that fulfillment" (Saint-Laurent 2000, 163). Thus Hinduism has a clear sense of the absolute in spite of the presence of numerous images. Above all gods there is the Absolute one who is not jealous.

b. The Universe

For the Hindu, the universe is neither good nor bad. Such are not the categories of their perspective of creation. In Hindu perception, in the long run, what may seem destructive (bad) or helpful (good) may not be so in the short term. The universe exists because it is influenced by God, who sustains it for a purpose. Yes, atoms and space constitute the universe, but there is a spiritual reality we must reckon with. After all, humanity is not simply physical, but spiritual as well.

After life comes death and decaying, but out of this comes life. Hindus are not enthusiastic about conquering nature (as most westerners). Rather, cooperating with nature is wisdom which leads to eternity. In Hindu thought, as seasons repeat themselves, so does the rest of nature. Theories such as the "big bang" only support belief in the Uncaused Cause because, before the *bang* was another *bang*, and prior to that there was a series of others, culminating in God - the reality that embraces all that we experience. Put differently, the origin of the universe is not spontaneous. There is a cause.

c. Humanity, Problems and Solutions

Hindu understanding of the human being starts with the Atman (the soul). A human being is the sum of the soul plus the "costume," i.e., the body which changes several times as the soul goes through the process of rebirth. According to this belief, the soul will reach the destiny just at it "originated" from it - with nothing but just the soul itself. Further, Hindus believe that the human being "reaps what he/she sows." Expressed as the Law of Karma, this belief is one of the most important doctrines. Simply stated: people get exactly what they deserve. Moreover, Hindus follow a sort of fatalistic belief which teaches that a human being cannot change the fact that they are what they are supposed to be, although there is a chance of one altering the future since everybody "reaps what they sow." Everyone is accountable for their actions.

Humanity faces one major challenge in Hindu concept of humankind, namely, reincarnation. The immortal soul will continue to inhabit one body after another until it is freed from the wheel of rebirth. Thus Karma does not end with physical death. Rather as long as the soul lives (though changing "costumes"), other forms of Karma are persistently generated. One's caste is the result of what one has done throughout life and, therefore, whatever is just is what the individual harvests. And, the individual always has a rare opportunity to influence one's life in the future by acting the right way in the present. Believing that what one does constitutes what one becomes, Hindus do not really need an external savior since all the components of their life's solutions are at their disposal, namely the soul, the law of Karma, the wheel of rebirth, and choice. Thus, according to this theology, it is within oneself to save one's life. Doing good is key!

d. Morality, Rituals and Symbols

Morality plays a major role in the Hindu community. Each soul aims to be reconciled with God. One has to overcome the "swinging pendulum" in order to strike the relationship with not just Karma or other persons, but also with Brahman. Full reconciliation occurs when Purusha is liberated from Prakriti, and Atman is liberated from Maya. Further, through *raja yoga*, the soul is liberated from the body; through *jnana yoga*, the mind is liberated from avidya so that it can perceive the truth of the universe. In *bhakti yoga*, the devotee is separated from materialism and becomes attached to God. Reconciliation results in serenity, identity, focusedness, and a noble sense of purpose. Thus, life's meaning is clear. Hindus believe that there is more than just one way to achieve reconciliation. One should seek a way that is suitable for one's personality. It is for this reason that several yoga types exist (as mentioned above). More importantly, as far as Hinduism is concerned, all these ways are of equal value. By the way, many Hindus also believe that, in addition to anybody choosing the way one prefers, one is at liberty to choose a deity who will assist him or her to "walk the walk." For example, the Vaishnavites will choose Vishnu who responds well to human petitions. Regarding Vishnu, one scholar notes:

> Vishnu, the almighty preserver and omnipresent protector of all things, is the most popular and benign of all Hindu gods. Vishnu possesses every gentle attribute, from benevolent kindness and fidelity to

overflowing compassion and sublime wisdom. Above all, Vishnu is a warm and loving God who cares deeply about the welfare of human beings. Vishnu abides constantly within the hearts of his devotees, and he may even manifest himself to them in visions (Saint-Laurent 2000, 174).

Shaivites will turn to Shiva, who is resourceful. Shiva is an awesome God of complex and paradoxical character in whom opposites strangely converge. In general, most gods are preferred for their power to promise immortality. And, typically, since most people choose to belong to some religion in order to be assured of security and immortality, they will choose such gods.

e.   Immortality

Hinduism believes that the soul is indestructible. The soul survives its body and moves on to another "host." This concept of samsara (reincarnation) has made Hinduism a unique religion. Life is a series of existence, a succession of existence. However, though the soul changes, it is of the essence of the Absolute (which does not change). Hindus believe that the soul *essentially* does not permanently change, in spite of all the metamorphosis it endures. There is difference of opinions among Hindu sages on whether a person can find eternal liberation in the physical body. But there is consensus that one who has lived life in "the approved paths can anticipate blessing one's family" as the family ancestor (Matthews 1999, 119).

Hinduism and its Sacred Scriptures

The term Hinduism is synonymous with Brahmanism, which originates from the Hindu priestly caste of Brahmins. Both terms refer to "the faith and the way of life" which has dominated the thought system of the majority of the people of India. Hinduism, which is based on the Vedas (i.e., Book of Knowledge), represents the early stages of Indian religion. Originally Hinduism was a sacrificial religion consisting of a multiplicity of deities as well as a pluralistic cosmology. Sanskrit, considered the ecclesiastical language of the educated Indians, constituted the Vedic literature. It is not surprising, therefore, that Sanskrit language is regarded as the classical religious vernacular and all religious texts have been written in that language from as early as 1500 B.C.E. According to Robert E. Van Voorst, the Hindu scriptures have been divided into two categories: 1. **Shruti**, which means "what is heard." This is the primary revelation. It has no human or divine author but captures the cosmic sounds of truth heard by the ancient seers; and 2. **Smriti**, which means "what is remembered" and is intended to designate all other scriptures (Van Voorst 2000, 25-26). From this Smriti category comes at least four Vedas, which laid the foundation of Hindu Scripture.

This religion that was born on the banks of the Indus River, is now embraced by almost one billion adherents. Due to a large following, one can expect Hinduism to now have varying interpretations and concepts of the "Hindu way of life." No one scholar could represent all the traditions in one book. Therefore, in this introduction to select major world religions, it suffices to only discuss general characteristics and beliefs of Hinduism. Although it is important to note that the original Dravidian communities (Pakistan) should claim to be the founders of Hinduism, it is essential to also introduce the Aryans (Indo-Europeans) who brought other religious ingredients and concepts from Persia and Greece. The Aryans, who believed that deities were the natural powers of heaven and earth, had learned early to give sacrifices to their gods, as well as share meals with their divinities by way of sacrificial offerings. This tradition intermingled with that of the Dravidian peoples, creating what became a very complex belief system.

Characteristic of most religions, the gods (devas) represented good things while the asuras represented evil. So the Hindu religion was to teach its followers to choose morality over immorality. Again, typical of other religions, Hinduism has always had a clearly defined ethical code. Thus, Hinduism as a religion developed as an interaction between the Dravidians and the Aryans. Historically, the light-colored Aryans assumed social superiority when they invaded and subdued the Dravidians who were dark-skinned, rendering the latter inferior. So *varna* (or color) played a decisive role in the development of what would be the caste system in Hinduism. We shall return to this topic for a fuller discussion later.

Another theory is that the Dravidians were a "civilized people" who were cultured and not as warring as the barbaric, power-hungry, insecure and domineering Aryan herders. So naturally, these (the Aryans) simply assumed superiority over the more submissive group. It seems that the tendency in insecure people is to be domineering in order to "be sure" they have full control of other groups.

It is instructive to also note that if the caste system is viewed by other religions as not humanizing, criticism need not discredit the religion as such since this philosophy does not constitute the basis of Hinduism. In Hinduism, caste is the permanent social group into which a person is born. One's social and religious obligations are determined for a lifetime by one's caste. Hindu devotees believe that one does not work one's way out of one's caste. Rather, he or she strives to meet all of life's obligations and responsibilities within the caste.

The Origins and Development of Hinduism

The Vedas - the Hindu sacred writings - is a major source of information regarding the origins and development of Hinduism. The Vedas itself is a record of the oral traditions which describe the story of Hinduism. Belonging to the category of the oldest religions of the world, Hinduism does not have a particular individual founder, as is the case with the three major religions of the Middle East crescent. The closest one gets to identifying the founder of Hinduism is when one describes the Dravidian people, a dark-skinned people who lived in cities along the banks of the Indus River.

Archaeologists have established that in this region there was a very advanced civilization. Although nothing decisive can be said about these people, it suffices to note that there are some resemblances between the old civilization and the present Hindu culture. There is also another component - the Aryans - a light-skinned people who moved in from Europe.

The Aryans who migrated from Greece, Persia and India, were of Ind-European background. They brought linguistic and religious concepts of Persia and Greece to the Indus natives. This community believed that deities were the natural powers of heaven and earth. As herders and pastoralists, the Aryans paid respects to their gods by sacrificing their livestock to the gods. The gods of the Aryans were believed to represent only those things which were good for human beings. Their beliefs, like most religions, served to regulate morality. Goodness is believed to triumph over evil. For this reason, a clear code of ethics was developed. We discuss some of this under the "Laws of Manu" below.

Somehow, as these two peoples intermingle - the dark-skinned Dravidian and the light-skinned Aryans - new methods and traditions of worship evolved. This must have influenced the rise of a new major religion - Hinduism - with its peculiar caste system. According to the varna theory, (skin pigmentation), since the light-skin people came as victors over the dark-skin people, there developed the belief that the light-skinned people were superior to the dark-skinned not only militarily but culturally as well. Another theory postulates that since the Aryans tended to be militant, domineering and aggressive, they automatically created a superior caste and placed themselves on a higher plane. However, the real permanent caste system had not been entrenched yet. But this could have been the beginning.

The Caste System

By definition, *caste* in Hinduism, describes the permanent social grouping into which a person is born, with social and religious obligations determined for a lifetime by caste. Put differently, there is no intermingling of castes. One is born into a caste where one is destined to belong. There are no biological or social errors.

Most scholars agree that the more widely accepted code of conduct is the "Laws of Manu" on the basis of which the caste system is constructed. The belief is that Manu is the primodal ancestor of humanity. Through Manu, various castes or classes in society received their moral codes, which date as far back as 200 B.C.E. The four major castes in Hinduism are namely the Brahmins, the Kshatriyas, the Vaishyas and the Shudras (priests, kings, commoners and shudras). The first three share a common characteristic; namely "being twice-born." The fourth and last is a not twice-born, thus removing it furthest from Brahman. Being twice-born suggests a higher rank toward purification or enlightenment.

In Hinduism, each person has specific duties according to one's stage in life. First is the student stage where, from between eight to twelve and not older than twenty-four, the young Hindu studies the Vedas. Carrying a sacred code on one's neck shows that one has been re-born spiritually. The youth studies under his or her *guru* for the rest of the duration from about twelve to twenty-four. The second stage involves getting married at twenty-five, and becoming a householder. The male must observe all the wisdom and ideals he learned under the guru because he is functionally, the "priest" of his family. Among the things to watch out for are: 1) avoiding unnecessary harm to any living thing, 2) observing all caste duties required of a married man, 3) carrying out all caste duties in one's profession, and 4) raising children. Entertaining guests and supporting holy men (e.g., monks and gurus) are other important obligations at this second stage. To wind up this stage, he hands over his caste duties and obligations to his son who will succeed him; hence, the importance of having a son.

The third stage - reflection stage - involves thinking and intellectualizing the "student duties" without actually executing them. At this stage, the man leans toward uniting with Brahman by removing himself from such material preoccupations like home, family, physical endeavors and all other earthly concerns. At least, most men regard this as retirement stage (retiring from the daily chores of a householder). Devotion to spiritual maturity receives priority.

The fourth and final stage is generally regarded as optional: *samahi*. This involves releasing one's soul so as to unite with Brahman. The Raja Yoga - a special psychology developed by the Hindus to train the body to be subservient to the soul - is undergone by men only. The ultimate goal is to have the Atman unite with Brahman.

Salvation in Most Religions in General

Most religions assure the adherents that if they observe all the doctrines and practices, generally they will experience salvation, defined as:

1. Deliverance from affliction; i.e., death, barrenness, misfortune, or sin;
2. Wholeness with respect to good health, peace of mind, integrated personality;
3. Deliverance from a disease, danger or any other peril which may either be a temporary measure or a permanent state.

Salvation is also defined in terms of permanent, long-term status. For instance, Christianity promised all those who believe in Jesus Christ that they will have "eternal salvation" - salvation through and beyond death. This form of salvation is generally understood as "life beyond this material existence." Such life is experienced in heaven, Paradise or the pure land. According to Buddhism, such liberation occurs in what the Buddhists call Nirvana. Salvation may also be understood as "a radical transformation" of the person. The individual does not understand how it happens but one certainly becomes aware that "life has changed" (of course for the better). Christians use the term "born again," most eastern religions talk of re-incarnation.

Salvation or deliverance is associated with attributes human beings long for, such as: long life, prosperity, progeny and of course, good health. It is for this reason that most religions "concentrate" on either the healing ministry, "prosperity gospel" or some such benevolence.

Furthermore, whether it is the Catholic church with its rosary, or Buddhism with the amulets of Buddha, or Judaism with its t'fillin (Torah box) on the arm of the adherent, respective believers expect spiritual, physical and psychological enhancement from the religion of their choice. Some religious leaders are known to have gone so far as to convince their followers that in order to "reap the benefits" of their faith, they have to die first (being persecuted, etc.). In some instances, this has been a *fatal* and *empty* promise. Generally speaking, most religions promise a more secure life after this physical state.

Salvation in Hinduism (in particular)

In Hinduism, these are the Four Ways of Salvation, set forth in the Bhagavad Gita.

Karma Yoga

This is the Way of Works. Krishna has praised this way of salvation in the Bhagavad Gita. Karma Yoga observed properly will lead to the goal of release (from the reincarnation of the soul). The most important practices include the Vedic sacrifices. According to this tradition, every household man has clearly defined duties. It is critical to remember to offer food to the gods, but most critical is performing rituals for the ancestors. Every household man is charged with the responsibility of nourishing the souls of the ancestors. Since women are not allowed to perform these rituals, for a couple to have a baby boy means a proper beginning of the family's liberation. Traditionally, this practice has resulted in the male child being preferred to a daughter in a Hindu family.

Of course, women have their own exclusive duties too. They are the ones who prepare the food used to feed the souls of the ancestors.

We cannot imagine how delicate this responsibility is. What if the food is rejected by the ancestors? That would spell disaster.

Jnana Yoga

Jnana Yoga means the Way of Knowledge. The Sankhya system of Hindu philosophy is dualistic. Its effect is to free *Atman* from *prakriti*. These two aspects of ultimate reality are experienced simultaneously. For a human being to alienate itself from God is only because of ignorance, not knowledge since the human soul itself is ultimately of the same essence as that of God. Unfortunately, in its ignorance, the human soul "thinks" that it belongs to the world which it ought to identify with, rather than identify with God from whom it originated. Consequently, each time the soul is reincarnated (rebirth), it suffers tremendously and each time it estranges itself from its vital force - its true nature and origin - more pain is self-inflicted. Because the human soul tries to "find itself" in the wrong places it can never establish its Way of Knowledge, which, alone, can overcome this detrimental ignorance. The truth that will set the human free is the enlightenment (knowledge) that the soul and the Brahman (God) belong together.

True liberation comes from the recognition of the reality that the human's soul does not belong (in terms of identity) to the world. Rather it is "grounded" in the Brahman - the ground of all being. When this realization occurs, immediately the soul (Atman) breaks away from the rebirth cycle into Nirvana, a state of total liberation, perfection, and contentment.

Bhakti Yoga

Bhakti Yoga means the Way of Devotion. This also is an important doctrine contained in the sacred Bhagavad Gita. According to this, serving God means embracing the Divine passionately in love. However, it is from the grace of God that much of the salvation comes from. The Hindu believes that no ritual, law or doctrine yields more saving power than God's grace. Therefore, in order to be preserved eternally by God, all one should do is devote oneself to God, trust God wholeheartedly and God's abundant grace will abound. A person who entrusts one's life in God cannot perish but have eternal life. Much of this teaching is based on the hymns - the Rig-Veda. This way of salvation clearly assures the adherent that there is life after death!

Bhakti was widespread among the masses of Hindus in India (300-600 CE). Here is a clear explanation of the *trimurti* beliefs, the triad of Gods: Brahman, Vishnu, and Shiva. Brahman (a God that may also appear in other Hindu gods) is one of the three gods. Brahma is attributed with creation. However, Brahman shares some responsibilities with the other God - Vishnu, the preserver God, and Shiva, the destroyer. It is also believed that Vishnu incarnated in the person of Krishna. Shiva destroys life in order to make room for other/new lives. However, Shiva can be generous to those who are devoted to him. It is interesting to note that in popular Hinduism most people prefer to serve either Vishnu or Shiva rather than the ultimate Brahman. Many Hindus have since incorporated Buddhism in Hinduism, believing that Siddhartha Gautama is the incarnation of Vishnu. More radical Hindus go as far as to incorporate Muhammad and Jesus (both founders of their respective religions) as incarnations of Vishnu.

Raja Yoga

Raja Yoga means the Way of Physical Discipline. The goal of Raja Yoga is to train the physical body to make the soul free. Rather than the body controlling the soul, this must control the physical body.

Samadhi comes after restraint of all physical and mental activity. According to the Bhagavad Gita, one should first develop an ethic that helps one to detach oneself from the world. To devote oneself to God seriously, one must control one's physical body, concentrate on cleanliness and self-control over physical desires. To accomplish this one concentrates on the *correct* bodily posture. (This means putting the body in a way where it ceases to be a concern.) Then one breathes correctly; i.e., in such a manner that the mind attains serenity. Next, all the senses should not be stimulated. The mind should be focused on one object until it fills the whole mind. Then remove that one object from filling the mind until the mind is empty leaving the mind blank (i.e., not conscious of that object). The final step involves extinguishes all consciousness of the world. These four: Karma Yoga, Jnana Yoga, Bhakti yoga and Raja Yoga provide the Hindus with four ways of salvation as they are set forth in the Bhagavad Gita. Following any of these will set the soul of the Hindu free. For each way, commitment, devotion and self-involvement play a very major role. Also, interaction with God and the cosmos is an important component. Thus, one can literally work on one's salvation. That is why Buddha taught: "Pull yourself like the elephant from the mud." Put differently, "Save yourself!"

The Role and Function of the Guru

Defined as "a Hindu teacher of religious duties," a guru "represents the divine in human form." The general sacred texts used by the gurus are the Upanishads. Gurus are also described more as "seers" than prophets. However, it must be made clear that gurus are not fortune-tellers, neither are they responsible for pronouncing doom or wrath from the gods upon the unfaithful. Unlike priests, gurus do not officiate at rituals - a matrix within which the gods are brought together with humans. Gurus are "thinkers" (philosophers) whose insights lead other people to believe that what they say is enlightenment from God. When a guru explains something to the student, the latter "sees in the teacher the very presence of the divine" (Matthews 1999, 90). Hearing truth spoken by the guru is like hearing God's truth through a human personality. Further, the guru's offering to the gods is one of the soul/mind, rather than one of materialism.

Although some gurus never marry, others do, and actually spend long hours teaching their sons and wives. Generally, gurus are abstemious: i.e., they live a simple life, without being preoccupied with materialism. Additionally, gurus renounce riches, food and alcohol. As far as the gurus are concerned, when they have knowledge they are wealthy. Enlightenment - understood as knowing that the soul is related to God, its ultimate origin - is the greatest wealth one will ever need. In Hinduism, the basic function of the guru is twofold. According to one authority, "He, of course, explains the scriptures, the spirit as well as the letter; but, what is more important still, he teaches by his life" (Swami Prabhavananda 1948, xi). Here is a good example of the life of a guru.

Yajnavalkya

Among their ranks, Yajnavalkya was one well-known guru. He had taught his wife the truth to such a degree that when the guru wanted to leave her with some material inheritance, Maitreyi (the wife) refused, preferring the knowledge of immortality. This incident triggered another thorough lecture by the guru. Regarding wisdom and truth, Yajnavalkya explained to his wife a series of concepts related to the meaning of self. The reason certain things are held dear to the human heart is because each such thing has the **self** in it. To know oneself is to understand the Being of the Universe, since the two are the same. This also triggered another concept: the idea of the Universe. One person asked a question regarding the foundation of existence: If space is the foundation of existence, then on what does space depend? In response, Yajnavalkya explained: on Brahman, which itself is the imperishable and is the ground of all being.

Brahman

Brahman is the most common name for the "ground of being" which sustains everything that exists. Even the Atman depends on the

Brahman. In fact, the two are essentially the same. The human Atman is virtually the same as that in every living creature. Hindu theology believes that the Atman ultimately becomes one with the Brahman. One's true identity lies in realizing that the Atman in me and the Brahman - the ground of all existence - are similar. Hinduism teaches that human beings are essentially spiritual, not physical. The closest kin of Atman is the Atman of all living things, which is grounded in the Brahman. When the Atman strives to be like Brahman it is only because it realizes that that is its origin - God. It is the Brahman (in me) seeking to "reunite" with the Brahman (out there). It is ultimately a mission on ultimate reunion. This is why the Upanishads states, "The secret of immortality is to be found in purification of the heart, in meditation, in realization of the identity of the self within and Brahman without; for immortality is union with God" (The Upanishads p. 13). Separation between the Atman and the Brahman is proved to be impermanent. What is ultimately permanent is the union between the Atman and the Brahman. That is a reason for everlasting enlightenment. Thus, life's struggle is for the Atman to be released from the body, which is impermanent, to unite with Brahman, which is permanent - this doctrine is known as Moksha.

Moksha

Moksha is one of the four major goals in Hindu life. Those weary of seeking other goals and now seek release from the wheel of rebirth altogether, choose the goal of Moksha. To reiterate, Moksha is only one of many ways to the one truth. The other ways include Karma, Artha and Dharma. A brief discussion of each of these will suffice.

The Karma

The *Law of Karma* states that every act, thought or deed, will have a consequence for future reincarnations. The Upanishads offer one more way for the individual to reach the God of the Universe. Karma can be defined as, "the inexorable principle in Hinduism that a person's thoughts and deeds are followed eventually by deserved pleasure or pain." The Upanishads are *shruti* - a form of revelation. Serious reflection on the *shruti* leads one to understanding God. It is no wonder various profound schools of thought (philosophies) have emerged from Hinduism. Some philosphies have monistic tendencies while others tend to be dualistic. What is believed to be true is that every person will ultimately be responsible for his or her acts and deeds. Since everything happens in the only one Universe, no one will escape this reality - the Law of Karma. Karma becomes clearer when we understand the philosophy of Monism, which is briefly stated here.

Monism

Monism is the view that there is only one fundamental reality. It is the opposite of the dualistic thinking that argues that there are two irreducible realities. The Chandogya Upanishad teaches unity of humanity and divinity. This is exemplified in the Brahman, which is "the ground of all being." As we have mentioned earlier, the human soul is the same in essence as the Brahman, its origin. This also leads to the doctrine of **Maya** which teaches that what appears to humans as ultimately different is, in fact, ultimately the same. Both these doctrines (the Monism and Maya) aim to underscore the doctrine of unity between the Atman and the Brahman. Hinduism's insistence on this unity prepares the adherent to become one with God, the creator.

Madhva's school of thought held an opposing view. According to Madhva's dualism, the relation of the self to Brahman and to the Universe is one of radical duality. The self is distinct from the Brahman, from other selves and from the world. Rather than via unity, the individual establishes a proper relationship to God by obedient service and faithful adoration.

Samsara

Samsara is the Hindu concept of the wheel of rebirth that turns almost forever. Souls are born again and again until they reach a state of perfection. The Upanishads, like the Vedas express an optimistic world view. For instance, they teach that life is good if one seeks goodness. An individual with bad karma continues to suffer when he or she is reborn in lower animals until a time when the individual is reborn in the Brahmin or priestly caste. According to the Samsara doctrine, the soul is reborn many times, each time in a body appropriate to the person's karma. The soul is permanent but it "goes through" and "wears" various bodies. The challenge to most Hindu thinkers is to ascertain how the soul can secure release from the cumbersome rebirth cycle.

On the whole, Samsara plays a critical role in Hindu theology. It teaches a principle of justice. Everything, whether it be good or evil, contributes towards how a person will be born in one's next life here on earth. Depending on one's quality of life (deeds, thoughts, actions, i.e., Karma), one may take a long time before being released from the series of reincarnation to being reborn in the Brahmin or priestly caste.

Further and finally, Samsara conveys the belief that the soul is reincarnated here on earth several times, depending on one's quality of life. Put differently, a person's Karma determines how many times one is to seek re-birth. Though the soul is believed to be permanent, in Hinduism, it changes hosts until the desired goal is achieved. Note that not all castes experience reincarnation. The Shudras (laborers) caste, the Vaishyas (merchants), and the Kshatriyas (the military) castes traditionally did not have equal access to Brahman, and therefore, lost enthusiasm. The reason being, from the, there was no end to reincarnation. This never-ending "suffering" necessitated the formation or discovery of other ways of finding release: for example, Jainism and Buddhism. Thus, these two religions were created out of frustration - the need for "The Way."

The Laws of Manu

Based on the fundamentals of the Laws of Manu, the Brahmins (priests) formulated and designed moral codes which lay out the moral standard for every Hindu caste. The Laws of Manu furnish us with an excellent description of the ideals of each caste. Every person knows what he or she ought to do or ought not do. One example of the Laws of Manu will suffice for our purpose here. It goes like this:

1. "Men must make their women dependent day and night, and keep under their own control those who are attached to sensory objects."
2. "Her father guards her in childhood, her husband guards her in youth, and her sons guard her in old age. A woman is not fit for independence."
3. "A father who does not give her away at the proper time should be blamed, and a husband who does not have sex with her at the proper time should be blamed; and the son who does not guard his mother when her husband is dead should be blamed." (Matthews 1999, 102-103).

One can obviously appreciate the clarity and systematic code which is only too difficult to violate.

However, since the law quoted above seems to pertain to men

only, making women seem "totally helpless," here is another side of the code - elevating women:

1. "Fathers, brothers, husbands, and brothers-in-law who wish for great good fortune should revere these women and adorn them."
2. "The deities delight in places where women are revered, but where women are not revered all rites are fruitless."
3. "Where the women of the family are miserable, the family is soon destroyed, but it always thrives where the women are not miserable."
4. "Homes that are cursed by women of the family who have not been treated with due reverence are completely destroyed, as if struck down by witchcraft."

"Therefore, men who wish to prosper should always revere these women with ornaments, clothes, and food at celebrations and festivals" (Matthews 1999, 103).

Although these laws are no longer observed or enforced strictly, there is general consensus that they still have a degree of influence among the Hindu of all castes. For Hindus who prefer to be conservative, this code is still a major moral pillar.

Topics for Research

1. What do you think about the caste system? Do you think it could be a form of racism? If so, what is the root of such racism? How does it compare to American racism?

2. What are your views on henotheism? What kind of god is the God in Hinduism?

3. Can a human being save oneself into eternal life? What is your personal opinion?

4. How does the Hindu concept of God compare to the concept of God in other religions like Judaism, Christianity, or Islam?

5. What are your views on fatalism, determinism, predestination, Atman?

Chapter 4

Buddhism

The ultimate goal of the religion known as Buddhism is to find the way to escape the pain of suffering in the world caused by constant rebirth and to enter *nirvana*. Buddhism is a universal religion that is non-theistic. (Buddhism is a spin-off from Hinduism.) It was revealed to the founder of Buddhism that *enlightenment* is the way of life. To understand Buddhism, let us first attempt to understand the life of Siddhartha Gautama, the prophet and charismatic founder of Buddhism.

The Life of the Founder

Around 560 BCE, at the foot of the Himalayas, was born a prince who became a prophet. King Suddhodanna and Queen Maya of the Shakya clan named their son Siddhartha Guatama. This young man grew up in luxury, shielded against the harsh reality of life and was given to extreme, sexual pleasures. Legend has it that Siddhartha's birth was brought forth by a sacred white elephant, which entered Queen Maya's womb and inserted the one who would be the Buddha. Such a birth was a *mystery*, which is one of the characteristics of major religions of the world. Due to this "mystery component" it is reasonable to assume that the birth of the Buddha unites with all other "births" designated as mysterious, thereby implying His Divine Commitment, participation and involvement. Certainly this "mystery component" is pregnant with theological content, which we will address later in this book. Suffice it to note that this Buddha is not just an ordinary person. He has a spiritual identity, which sets him apart as a divine vessel. It is no wonder many authorities describe him thus: "During the remainder of his eighty years he was revered as Shakyamuni, the sage of the Shakyas, and as the compassionate Buddha" (Matthews 1999, 127).

Siddhartha went through the Brahmanical steps (i.e., Hindu) as a student. At 19 years, he married a neighboring princess, Yoshodhara. The couple had a son, Rahula. According to Brahmanic customs, Siddhartha had fulfilled his duty as a responsible Hindu. He had met all the qualifications for a Kshatriya caste, but because he did not mingle with the community, he did not know what life was all about, until one day!

Siddhartha lived a sheltered life. When he explored the world "beyond the palace," on four different occasions, he saw four sights that deeply affected him:

1. First, he saw an old man. . .so old, that it made Siddhartha aware that youth does not last forever! In fact, old age was characterized by misery. The beauty of youth is impermanent!
2. Second, he saw a sick person. . .so sick that Siddhartha realized that sickness and suffering are part of human existence. Good health is not to be taken for granted.
3. AS if these two sights were not enough, Siddhartha actually saw a corpse. . .a funeral procession (a mourning crowd). They were burying the dead. Siddhartha learned that death befalls every human - rich or poor, king or servant, young or old, educated or uneducated. This experience was a rude awakening for the hitherto sheltered prince.
4. Siddhartha was greatly relieved when he saw a wandering ascetic. The wandering monk. . .simple, happy and worry-free, offered the solution. In Siddhartha's thoughts, this significantly influenced his life. He decided to abandon all materialism in pursuit of asceticism/spirituality. This was the only way to deal with human suffering. Needless to say, this shattered his father's expectation of the prince! But Siddhartha would not turn back. He had committed his life to the highest ideal.

The Great Enlightenment

At 29, Siddhartha literally abandoned his wife, son, and the entire princely life. He was on the path to seek release from the constant suffering from the wheel of rebirth. He shaved his head, acquired the attire of an ascetic and left home as a wanderer (an ascetic). He chose to study under two gurus, one after another. These gurus tried to teach him, through intellectual order, the way to the realm of nothingness. Unsatisfied, Siddhartha left and tried more rigorous asceticism, such as practiced by Jainas.

In Siddhartha's thinking, as long as one continues to enjoy the pleasures of the flesh, one cannot find the light of truth (or release from reincarnation). Siddhartha did everything to make himself miserable by starving himself, living so simply that all that was left was to die! In fact, tradition has it that he got to the point of being unconscious until a certain village maid, Sujata, gave a little food which brought him back to life! Then Siddhartha concluded that such extreme asceticism was not really effective. It had not brought release fro the wheel of rebirth, but had actually led to more suffering.

Having exhausted all traditional ways of meditation, Siddhartha sat under the Bo tree, the tree of enlightenment. There it happened. He received the enlightenment that he had been seeking. To this day, a temple, Bodhgaya (memorial temple) has been erected at this site. Here he found knowledge, which dispelled ignorance. Siddhartha discovered that by destroying *desires*, he would eliminate suffering. This would:
1. Set him free,
2. Make him awake,
3. Make him enlightened, and
4. Lead him into Nirvana.

The evil one, Mara, tempted Siddhartha while he was going through this search for enlightenment. For instance, Siddhartha was tempted to go back to his old princely living, to his Kshatriya duties (family), but he overcame every temptation.

When Siddhartha overcame the temptor, he received blessings from the gods. According to tradition, the Buddha remained under the Bo tree for almost seven weeks. Siddhartha had gained knowledge of release from rebirth. Filled with joy, compassion and enlightenment, the Buddha went out to share the good news. So, he started to teach. Buddhism was born. The prophet - the Buddha - started to develop a doctrine, concepts and ways of formulating *truth*.

The Four Noble Truths

Buddha taught his followers that there are four aspects of realization necessary for anyone to achieve enlightenment. These are (in the Sanskrit language):
1. Dukkha - suffering,

2. Samudaya - suffering has a cause,
3. Nirodha - cessation of suffering, and
4. Marga - the Way.

The Marga is also known as the Way because, after following the Eightfold Path to Liberation, one completely overcomes suffering and achieves the state of *nirvana*.

Now, let us briefly discuss each of the *four noble truths.*

a.   Dukkha

Dukkha is the Noble Truth of being *unsatisfactory* - nothing is really satisfactory. This teaching does not render Buddhism pessimistic - Buddha did not teach pessimism. He simply taught that we are to be realistic. We must acknowledge that there is persistent suffering in life. The most obvious example of suffering is sickness and death. Buddha teaches that all things are impermanent. Those who are fortunate enough not to experience sickness and death should also know that, sooner or later, all their leisure will cease. Everything is impermanent. Beauty, youth, newness, riches, poverty, etc., will all come to an end one day. Furthermore, what we desire at one point becomes most undesirable at another point.

Everything is temporary and exists only conditionally. Buddha believes that, generally, we suffer from not being able to gratify in full our desires. There is also a sense of uneasiness that originates from not being able to fully know or understand who and what we are. We are unable to identify ourselves with any precision. Fortunately, there is something that counter-balances this more-or-less pessimistic view of life, which is the second Noble Truth.

b.   Samudaya

Samudaya is the second Noble Truth that Buddha taught. The endless suffering which Buddha has identified actually has a cause. One needs to realized the cause of this suffering which makes everything temporary. The suffering of humanity is not an inherited characteristic of human nature. We bring it upon ourselves by desiring what we do not fully comprehend.

c.   Nirodha

Nirodha is the cessation of suffering. Suffering, like all other things, is impermanent. Also, there is a time to suffer and a time not to suffer. One may eliminate suffering through certain yogic practices. When suffering is eliminated completely, one has achieved Nirvana. Apart from causing suffering to end through certain practices, one may also end suffering eventually as all seasons gradually come to an end.

d. Marga

Marga is the fourth Noble Truth. Marga means "The Way," i.e., the way out of suffering, the way to Liberation, the way to Nirvana. Marga is the way to Enlightenment. Siddhartha's experience was that there is an Eightfold Path to achieving *The Way*. The Eightfold Path consists of a series of interconnected components, namely:
Right View
Right Aspiration
Right Speech
Right Conduct
Right Livelihood
Right Effort
Right Mindfulness
Right Contemplation

These do not occur sequentially, but gradually and simultaneously, leading to the attainment of Enlightenment or Liberation. However, all eight components must be present to fulfill the rationale. Each component serves a purpose that the others cannot. For instance, Right View means the possession of the right perspective with respect to reality. Right View also means having a religious experience of some sort, leading to a clearer comprehension of what life is really about. Three components actually belong together (Right View, Right Aspiration, and Right Thought) under the rubric of wisdom. Another cluster (Right Action, Right Livelihood and Right Speech) belongs under the rubric of morality. These constitute the doctrine of moral conduct, which one finds in almost every major religion.

This Right Action cluster consists of not harming, killing, committing adultery...all kinds of behavior which would be injurious to other human beings. These "Rights" also help the individual to achieve Enlightenment, especially as one fulfills the karmic theory according to "what goes around comes around." In fact, moral prohibition has a central role in Buddhism. Like other forms of eastern religions, Buddhism seeks harmony with nature - that is life.

The Buddhists believe that a stable mind is crucial for self-control. So, the Right Effort and Right Mindfulness both have to do with training the mind to concentrate and control sensations, emotions and thought. In sum, Buddhism places a lot of premium on the person - self-control.

The Self

Buddha's decision to sever relations with Hinduism was principally influenced by his doctrine of impermanence. Where Hinduism had taught that everything except the human soul (Atman) changes and is impermanent, Buddha taught that, based on his enlightenment, everything *including the Atman* is impermanent.

Furthermore, Buddha argued that since it is the soul/self (Atman) that moves from body to body (causing constant rebirths), it too *changes*. Buddha's target was to "destroy" the concept of *ego* ("me" - self-centeredness). In his view, the "I" causes a lot of dislikes and likes and when these are not met, suffering occurs. Buddha further questioned/challenged the importance of this "I" whose abode cannot even be located. [It is the heart or the mind that desires?] So, Buddha's theology seeks to destroy the "I-ness" which causes heartache.

The second reason Buddha sought enlightenment is that "the things of existence do no exist in a set, dualistic hierarchy of 'real' and 'unreal'." For Buddha, the human being does not consist of external components, such as the soul. What other philosophies Iplato's) and theologies (St. Augustine) call the "soul" or "ego," Buddha merely perceived as "a profound level of consciousness." This quality, no matter how abstract, is - may be - still remains - changeable and impermanent. Buddha denies the concept of total self-dermination. He argues that we can never really fully detach ourselves from everything else that is a part of the Universe. We are responsible for what happens in ouor world because we are *of the world*. For instance, Buddha argues that the individual derives from two parents whom, themselves, belonged to their parents, and so on, ad infinitum. At any given point in time, the individual's genealogical make-up draws from infinite generations past and will constitute future, endless generations. He further believes that in addition to our genealogical make-up are, the components of the food we eat, the air we breathe, the water we drink, the sunlight we absorb, and so on. Furthermore, we are made up of our environment - television programs, enemies, emotions, family, and all.

In sumary, the Buddhist believes that each living being is an extremely complex combination of factors. There is no single entity which is by itself determinative. So why should the "I" seem to stand on its own? Why does the "I" purport to be independent of all else? Buddha's answer to these rhetorical questions is: "The 'I' is only part of the universe."

The Concept of Karma

The concept of Karma is very crucial in Buddhist understanding of humanity. Buddhism teaches that all living beings are nothing but Karma. Human beings (as well as other creatures) are forever trapped in a cyclical existence, known as Samsara. A human being is thought of as a cluster of countless Karmas from the external past, now manifesting itself as a mighty river of Karma. It is this Karma that allows for the appearance of distrinctive and relatively constant phenomena that tends to give the appearance of an immutable self.

Indeed the role of Karma performs a complete role in the development of what a living being will turn into in the future. There is no unchanging external ego within living beings. We are all nothing more than Karma. At birth, some people seem to hve some natural abilities. Ths should not surprise us because the living being has been cultivating its abilities over many lives through which it has gone.

Compassion and Wisdom

The Mahayana movement developed the concpet of emptiness with its hero, the *bodhisattva*. This term literally means, "enlightened being." Though a little less than the Buddhahood stage, the bodhisattva is quite advanced in its perfection. Thus, at this stage, one hasdeveloped a remarkable degree of compassion. The bodhisattva follows a new program different from the Eightfold Path to Liberation. This is known as the *paramitas*, which consists of "six perfections," namely:
1. The Perfection of Giving,
2. The Perfection of Morality,
3. The Perfection of Patience,
4. The Perfection of Effort,
5. The Perfection of Concentration, and
6. The Perfection of Wisdom.

Briefly, the *perfection of giving* entails *willingness* to donate one's physical, mental and spiritual assets without any thought of recompense. *Perfection of morality* involves the implementation of the traditional Eightfold Path of Liberation.

However, this is based on the understanding that all objects of desire are empty because all things are empty. The *perfection of patience* leads to a state of mind, which is dominated by equanimity - everything is equally empty. Nothing should excite one. This is also supported by the *perfection of concentration*. Furthermore, one should strive toward enlightened existence. The most critical one is *perfection of wisdom*. Wisdom refers to the ability to penetrate to the true mature of all things based on the experienceof emptiness. This last one is necessary in order for the others to be fruitful and realistic. What we have said of wisdom is also true of compassion. The vision of all things as empty allows the bodhisattva to practice the *perfection of giving* since one is, at this stage, no longer attached to any possessions. Compassion makes wisdom possible while, at once, wisdom is enhanced by compassion.

Buddhism: Development After the Founder's Death

There are two ways through which one can *experience* the Buddha. One way is the tradition of the elders - the Theravadins, a group that follows the path of the monks who lived a strictly monastic life. Theravadins are directed toward Nirvana. The other gorup is known as the Mahayanists who revered the Three Jewels and envisioned a larger order which included both laypersons and monks. The question arose, of the two groups (The Theravadians and the Mayayanists) who was closer to the Buddha? In pursuing this dispute, these two schools of thought have emerged suggesting that both branches are vital paths to liberation. Or, do they?

a. ***Theravadins***

The Theravadins severed relations with the Mahayana based on where one placed emphasis regarding the life of the Buddha. What we may designate as the conservative school of thought focused on how Buddha lived his life. They favored imitating the founder in asceticism. One of the major characteristics of the Buddha which the Theravidians would imitate, is the belief that one should"pull oneself out of the mud" - i.e. working out one's own salvation by right aspiration and right meditation. According to the Theravadins, one becomes an arhat When one attains supreme enlightenment. Not only are monks required to spend long periods of time in the monastery, laypersons are also expected to spend some time in concentrated meditation. Monks live on one meager meal per day, given by any faithful laity in the community. Monks whose lifestyle was admired by most got more food than did less popular monks.

Theravadins began as very conservative, but with time, they have relaxed some of their self-imposed restrictions. Their memory of Buddha is symbolized by a footprint or an empty throne, or a stupa for relics. With time, even images of the Buddha wre permitted. *Jatakas* (stories of the prophet's previous life) were also eventually permitted. One of their eschatological beliefs is that the Buddha who awaits in the *Tusita* heaven will one day descend to the earth at the eschaton.

Those who cannot imagine who the Buddha was, are contended to imitate the monks who themselves are assumed to be following the steps of the Buddha. Whether one follows the prophet or a monk, the central, undergirding belief is that salvation come through dedicatged self-effort. There is no savior from out there. This is possible because the Buddha is always quoted to have said: "Pull yourself from the mud like an elephant." This is the salvific message. But the other branch of Buddhism holds a different view.

b.   *Mahayana*

The Mahayanists regard themselves as the greater vehicle. This branch believes in a wider range of possibilities. Also, their role models are quite diverse. The Mahayana believe that they have advanced beyond what the Buddha taught and so do not confine their practice to literal interpretations of the prophet's teaching. The Mahayanists identify themselves with the superior teachings to which the prophet pointed them.

One of the major beliefs which clearly distinguishes this school of thought from the Theravadins is the concept of heavenly being swho are able to assist human beings to escape from suffering in order to enter a more beautiful sphere beyond the grave. However, the Bodhisattvas (heavenly beings) whose task is helping humans to enter Nirvana, themselves remain outside Nirvana. Another belief is that soon after his death, Siddhartha Gautama grew to be more than a human monk. For this branch, salvation is not just a matter of what one can do to "pull oneself from the mud." There is also need for redemption brought by "a plethora of enlightend heavenly beings" always ready to assist finite human beings. Actualy these "heavenly beings" are described as variations of Buddhas assigned to assist every generation just as Gautama helped his generation. Moreover, there is a sense in shich everyone is a potential Buddha.

Some Commonalities and Differences (between Theravadins and Mahayanists)

Since the two schools of Buddhism share a common ancestry, it is evident that there are some commonalities; yet, due to the fact that they are two different schools, there must be some differences. Here are a few examples:

1. Mahayanists favord wide participation whereas Theravadins preferred only a select group, namely those who observe the monastic ideal. They believed that by following the steps of the Buddha as individuals, they could workout their own experiences of enlightenment (Nirvana). The issue was the means of salvation.
2. Mahayansists found merit in deeds. Giving food, clothing, medicines, and shelter would certainly be meritorious and rewarded. Further, they belileved that the relics of the Buddha scantened everywhere retained the Buddha power. Thus Buddha was conceived as eternal. Therefore, he would continue to respond to their suffering. Mahayanists were outgoing, had a sense of sharing and bieng in community with those gone beyond. The Theravadins looked withng themselves iln meditation and renounced metaphysics.
3. Mahayanists preferred to communicate with the Buddha who is now liberated from the confines of a body, while the Theravadins slavishly imitate the earthly Buddha. The issue was authority or originality.
4. One clear commonality is that both the Theravadins and the Mahayanists were Buddhists - inspired by the Buddha. The is ultimate religous identity.
5. The Theravadins spread over the south and east Inda; while the Mahayanists stretched north, then east and west. The question of missionary activity.
6. They each developed schools where their respective teachings and philosophies were taught. (Interested researchers may look up these items: a) The Madhyamika school ((Nagarjuna), b) the Yogacara school (Maintreyanatha), c) King Ashoka (273 - 232 B.C.E.) and Buddhist misionary activities.

In conclusion, like other major religions of the world, although

Buddhism developed two or more branches, it did not lose its identity as a religion. There is enough thread to help Buddhism maintain its identity.

Chapter 5

Taoism

Taoism is one of China's several indigenous religions. Other eastern religions include Confucianism, Buddhism, the state cult of China and the folk religion of China. Two features characterize any of these religions of China:
1. Religion is the pursuit of harmony.
2. Religion is not a separate compartment of life. It is integrated into family, government, medicine/health, and other aspects of everyday existence.

The Chinese have always conceived of unity between heaven, earth, human beings, and all other spiritual forces. To upset one aspect of life disturbs the whole cosmos; for instance, sin committed by an individual has cosmic implications. Ancestors, i.e., the living-dead are part of the living, as well as the spirit world. In fact, they actually influence the life of the living. All this interconnectedness leads to a harmonious worldview. Human beings must live in harmony with the cosmos to avoid disasters. This is what every one of these religions teaches. Now, let us focus on one such religion - Taoism.

Taoist Beliefs

Taoism is a religion based on the Tao Te Ching - sacred literature traditionally attributed a Chinese safge, Lao-Tzu, who lived in the sixth century BCE.

Tao is defined as "the mysterious source and order principle underlyilng all that is" (Patterns of Religion, 1999). Tao is believed to be more fundamental than any divine being. The Tao is experienced as female because its primary funciton is to nurture and sustain all that is. It is the Ultimate Source. Furthermore, Tao is likened to a mother (not a father). Tao is conceived as the very origin of all reality. Everything comes from the Tao, even the world! Taoists believe in the creation process known as "self-generation." Nothing caused the Tao to be - no external reality brought the Tao into being. The tao grows itsef in the Universe, making the world the body of the Tao. The universal body is also coneived as the body of Lao Tzu. So viewed, the anatomy of the universe is named as follows:

The Sun = Lao Tzu's left eye
The moon = Lao Tzu's right eye
The K'un-lun mountain = Lao Tzu's head
The planets = Lao Tzu's beard
The snakes = Lao Tzu's bowels

Taoists believe that the cosmic Lao Tzu is an androgynous being who is identical with his mother. The world is actually a single organism - the cosmic, androgynous Lao Tzu. Understood this way, the mroe perfect the harmony, the better the universe.

The Taoist Cosmos

The Tao itself can be regarded as a "Zero" since it is neither positive nor negative. Rather, it is perceived as "potential.:" All creation originates from the *Ch'i* - a breath of life. Each human being has this *Ch'i*, whose purpose is to "nurture their vital breath." In a summary, here is how the sacred literature states the process of gestation of the cosmos:

"The Way (Tao) gave birth to One;
The One gave birth to Two;
The Two gave birth to Three;
And the Three gave birth to the ten thousand things."

(Note, in Chinese, "ten thousand" is symbolized to connote everything!)

For the Taoists, everything - every event - can be understood as either the yin or the yang or both. The "yin" type of energy is characterized as dark, cook, we, obscure, female, passive, earth, and death. The "yang" is depicted as the opposite, characterized as light, dry, male, warm, active, heaven, and life. Taoists must learn how to manage Ch'i in order to be on the path of light (male) onto heaven, where the "yang" leads. However, the Taoists believe that there can be no "yang" without the "yin," just as there canot be the "yin" without its complementary components. Consequently, Taoists embrace both components in order to accomplish the desired goal, namely cosmic harmony.

In Taoist theology, the gods were formed after the heavens. In fact, these are personal manifestations of the Tao. Human beings feature somewhere between the heaven and the earth and are the most potent of all creation. Human conditions tend to wear out the Ch'i, however, this can be checked and even reversed. Human beings can choose to expend their energies or to capitalize on them so as to save themselves. As pointed out at the beginning of this chapter, human behavior can influence the entire cosmos insofar as it is triggered by components of the whole. Our behavior can eith destroy or renew harmony. Put differently, the fate of the universe depends on oour morality. Therefore, a sound morality has tremendous value to not only society, but the entire cosmos.

For Taoist, each person is a microcosm constituting a whole universe - a macrocosm. Nothing stands in isolation. Everything is connected to everything else. Unfortunately, only the enlightened people can comprehend this concept, and those who do have a key to well-being and even immortality.

Again, it is crucial to understand the Taoist theology of humanity and anthropology - every human is a microcosm of the universe. This concept of "things" sheds light on Taoist practice and Chinese culture in general.

Divinities

In Taoism, four major types of spiritual beings are recognized.
1. Gods,
2. Immortals,
3. Ancestor Spirits, and
4. Demons.

Of these, gods are attributed with both omnipotence and the power to save humanity. Creation is attributed to the Tao, however - not gods. Principal among all the gods is a group of three, known as tshe *Pure Ones*, or Worthies, or Lords. The *Lord of Heaven's* sphere of influence in the microcosm of the human being is the head. The Numinous treasure Heavenly worthy, who is the *Lord of Earth* and has jurisdiction over the human heart or chest. The third member - the Heavenly Worthy of the Way - is the *Lord of Humanity* with dominion over the human abdomen.

This Lord of Humanity is the deity believed to have incarnated into a human form becoming the sage, Lao Tsu. It is to him that the Tao Te Ching is attributed.

Immortal spiritual beings are believed to be mysterious. Somehow they attained transcendent condition as a result of practicing Taoism. These seem to be the mose independent among all the Taoist spiritual members of the community. The immortals are the model of human perfection in Taoism. They are beings who possess etherealized form of body, linking their spiritual to their physical dimensions. Two types of immortals exist: The heavenly and the terrestrials. At any time, the immortals can change their shapes, becomin invisible or appear as hermaphrodites. However, when they are among mortals, as a rule, they "take on" the color of ordinary human beings in order to be camouflaged. For the most part, immortals' actions show unconditional benevolence toward human beings.

The ancestor spirits, unlike the immortals, can either be benevolent or malevolent. The Taoists believe that if a person dies a violent death - say automobile accident - the spirit may becom "demonic." The Taoist priestes, however, can exorcise such demons.

Taoist belief in the spirit-world draws a clear distinction between the gods of folk religion and the Worthies. Criteria for differentiation are: origin, potency, and place of abode. Taoist gods are believed to be extermely powerful. On the other hand, the gods of folk religion trace their origin from humanity. They were once human beings who then rose to divine status. By contract, Taoist gods are thought of as special divine manifestations of the Tao. Furthermore, Taoist gods reside in the higher heavenly realms, whereas the gods of folk religion have their abode either in "Lower Heaven" or even on Earth! Locating the Toaist gods in higher heavens need not signify remoteness. Rather, it indicates significant status and power. We conclude with a summary note that, whereas some Taoist gods are worshipped in folk religion (for instance, the Jade Emperor), Taoists do not worship gods of folk religion.

The Nature of Humanity

Taoism teaches that every human being possesses the Chi'i, a primal energy that can make it possible for them to attain salvation. Humans are a microcosm of the universe; consequently, they are regarded as manifestations of the *One* - the original eternal energy. This *One* is what is referred to within every human being as either the real self, the real one, the immortal embryo, or the divine Ch'i of La-Tzu. However, although everyone has this Ch'i, not everyone can become immortal. Some people choose not to utilize and realize this potential. The body contains "three worms" (Three Corpses) which lure a person to lust and gluttony, which brings early death. The three worms keep track of one's sins, report to heaven (if reports are negative) - and life may be shortened. Taoists believe that demons may reside in a person, particularly when the individual's personality is made weak by misdeeds.

According to Taoism, each person's body contains thirty-six thousands gods, not counting the *One*. These serve to counter the negative forces (the demons) that surround and seek to attack us. This belief in thousands of gods is comparable to the macrocosm, which contains a myriad of gods. These gods (in the human body) feed on the purest nutrients - saliva and breath. Note that among all the food we eat, the gods detest meat and wine. Also, the three *Pure Ones* can be invoked to invigorate the person as well as ward off demons.

Taoist Practice and Morality (Ethics)

Like in many religions, Taoism teaches morality, which is enforced by the priestes - the Tao-shih. The ordinary people - the Tao-min, expect to be guided by the Tao-shih. For most adherents, Taoist rituals bring together and embody Taoist beliefs in the most powerful manner. The most common rituals are the Chiao (rite of cosmic renewal) and the Chai (fast). The overall goal of Taoist practice is a morality that causes harmony to be the status quo.

Taoist morality can be expressed in a word: *altruism*. This morality is based on two fundamental principles; namely, 1) Wu-Wei (non action) and Te (virtue), and 2) Performing specific good works in a wide range of social and environmental contexts.

All Taoist action is informed by Wu-Wei. Generally, this means that one should refrain from action - especially from forced, phony and blatantly aggressive action. One shold refrain from willful, selfish action. Wu-wei implies a natural way of functioning - "going with the flow" as it were. One must act in accordance with the Tao-nature. This is achieved through profound intuition of the inter-relatedness of all things.

Finally, Taoism, like many other religious traditions, calls for benevolence, compassion and humility. Like others, it prohibits murder, stealing and lying. Concer for the poor, the orphans, the widows, the elderly and the children is also part of Taoist morality.

Topics for Research

1. Compare and contrast Taoism with folk religion with specific reference to the gods, the priests and humanity.

2. Construct a theology of Taoism, based on the religious concepts and practices of Taoism.

3. Discuss all aspects of Taoism which are attributed to Lao-Tzu.

4. How does Taoism deal with the problem of evil?

5. Discuss and trace the influence of Taoism throughout not only China but also the whole world.

Chapter 6

Judaism

The Rise of Judaism: An Overview

The first ancestors (Patriarchs) of Judaism received the revelation from God in Mesopotamia (1800 B.C.E.) about 4000 years ago. Thus, the history of Judaism begins and ends with God who called Abraham to be "God's follower." Abraham had sons - Isaac who would be the Father of Israel, and Ishmael who would be the Patriarch of the Arab world. Jacob, Isaac's son had Joseph in addition to eleven other sons. Events according to God's plan led Joseph being sold as a slave to some merchants traveling to Egypt, where he eventually became the Pharaoh's deputy, developed Egypt's agricultural policies to the point where only Egypt had not only sufficient but surplus grain during a major famine that brought the Hebrews to Egypt to buy grain. Here, Jacob's whole family found itself at the mercy of the brother they had 'sold away into slavery and nothingness." With time, the Hebrews were enslaved by the Egyptians, but Moses, one of the Hebrew sons, was asked by God to lead his people out of bondage, to a land of freedom which God gave them. Again, this proved God's faithfulness to Abraham and his offspring according to the covenant.

The rise and development of Judaism is characterized by two components: the historical (community) and the theological (God). Jewish history is consistent with, and can only be understood in the light of the will of God.. Thus, the Tanakh, especially the Torah, is nothing but a record of what God said and did including the creation of the universe, the liberation of Israel from the Egyptian bondage and all that constitutes Israel's' politics, government, morality, leadership, survival and national identity. It is no wonder the Hebrew state was generally described as a theocracy - government by God. Put differently, the history of the Hebrews is sometimes described as the history of salvation.

The Patriarchs and the Covenant

When God appeared to Abraham in the third millennium B.C.E. in Haran, God challenged him to follow divine instructions and observe God's promises. Abraham, the son of Terah, of the city of Ur, was charged to emigrate to the land surrounding the Sea of Galilee. God also promised Abraham to be the father of nations:

> "I will make of you a great nation, and I will bless you; I will make your name great; and you shall be a blessing." (Genesis 12:2)

Evidently, Abraham only agreed to emigrate (from his native land) because he had faith in God. Accompanied by Lot, his cousin, Abraham relocated and began a nomadic life among the indigenous people. The main difference between Abraham and the rest of the community was that he was here by God's design whereas the other people had always been there. Most likely, Abraham was more God-conscious than his neighbors. Further, there was a special covenant between God and Abraham. To be sure there would be no mix up, Abraham decided that all his sons, grandsons and the rest of the male posterity would bear a sign by way of circumcision. Many scholars agree that the covenant between God and Abraham was more than just a mere contract because it was without date of expiration. In addition to circumcision, Abraham and his descendents committed themselves to always prepare a sacrifice to God.

As noted earlier, Isaac had his own sons, Esau and Jacob. Ishmael, a son born to Abraham and Hagar, (Sarah's maid), eventually left home and was forced to live in Arabia. To date Ishmael is revered as leader of the Arabs. God's covenant with Abraham was conveyed to Jacob through Isaac. The former had twelve sons who became the heads of the twelve tribes of the Israelites. Long after the death of Joseph, new pharaohs ruled Egypt and had neither knowledge of nor respect for Joseph and his descendents. So, a decree to enslave the Hebrews, slaughter all male children and torture the Hebrews was enacted. The Hebrew people began to suffer immensely.

One thing in favor of the Jews is that they were permitted to keep their own culture as much as they wanted, and to worship a God of their choice. Slavery intensified. Suffering got worse until God was moved to "come down and liberate" God's own people whom God had promised to take good care of (Exodus 3). So, God sent Moses to face Pharaoh and demand that Pharaoh let the Hebrews go free. Many scholars tend to concur on the view that the Pharaoh in question - who is described as the toughest - must have been Rams II, of the nineteenth dynasty (1290-1244

B.C.E.). But the main point is that this pharaoh had no regard, respect or feelings for the Hebrew people. He actually viewed them as a menace.

Divine Deliverance

a. Political

God chose Moses to lead the Hebrews from the Egyptian bondage. Scholars generally believe that it is the same Moses who wrote the Pentateuch, including the Ten Commandments. Moses had been saved miraculously from Pharaoh's decree to have all male children among the Hebrews killed. His mother had hid him when Pharaoh's daughter "found" him and took him home (Pharaoh's Palace) where he was educated just like a prince should. After being involved in a couple of fights, Moses felt that that he was not an Egyptian but a Hebrew had become common knowledge. So, he fled to Midian, where God later revealed Godself to him, empowering him to go back and face Pharaoh (Exodus 3:2-10). Whenever Moses was in a very critical situation, he would call on God who had given him the power "to talk to Pharaoh" and say: "Let my people go!" However, such a move involved the Holy Ghost power because Pharaoh was stubborn.

Moses had to inflict a series of plagues on the Egyptians in order to impress upon them the urgency of the matter. The tenth plague "moved Pharaoh" to finally let them go. When God sent his angel to kill all Egyptian firstborn sons, and spare the Hebrew first born, Egypt finally lost the war. This event - when the people of Israel were saved - is the famous Passover which commemorates the liberation of the Hebrews from slavery. The ritual involved slaughtering a lamb and smearing the blood on the door post of every Hebrew house so that when the angel of death came at night, he would "pass over" (spare) the Hebrews but enter the Egyptian homes which, of course, did not have this "password". Released, the Hebrews left Egypt, headed north, crossed the Red Sea by the Power of God which drowned the Egyptian soldiers and their chariots who sought to recapture them. The Hebrews headed toward the Land of Canaan via Mount Sinai. The journey through the desert would take them forty years!

b. Spiritual

God gave Moses the laws which the people were to live by. Popularly known as the "Ten Commandments" or the decalogue, these laws did much to mold the peole of Israel as one community that believes in one God. In fact, the people of Israel literally carried the <u>The Ark of the Covenant</u> (a large box) believing that carrying it wherever they went constituted "obeying" God's law. The Ten Commandments as recorded in Exodus 20:2-17, state as follows:

1. You shall have no other gods besides Me.

2. You shall not make for yourself a sculptured image, or any likeness of what is in the heavens above, or on the earth below, or in the waters under the earth.

3. You shall not swear falsely by the name of the Lord your God; for the Lord will not acquit one who swears falsely by His name.

4. Remember the Sabbath Day and keep it holy.

5. Honor your father and mother, that you may long endure on the land that the Lord your God is assigning to you.

6. You shall not murder.

7. You shall not commit adultery.

8. You shall not steal

9. You shall not bear false witness against your neighbor.

10. You shall not covet your neighbor's house; you shall not covet your neighbor's wife, or his male or female slave, or his ox or his ass, or anything that is your neighbor's.

Failing to keep the commandments resulted in punishment that could extend to several generations. Rewards for observing the law also extended to posterity. The books believed to have been authored by Moses, include: Exodus, Leviticus, Numbers, and Deuteronomy, and are known as the Torah (the Law). Genesis, the first book of the Bible, describes the creation, humanity, and the cosmos. This, too, is attributed to Moses' authorship. The Pentateuch constitutes a very crucial aspect of Jewish faith and politics. Much of their worldview and theology is prescribed here.

c. Doctrine of Judaism

Judaism teaches that the Lord God is One. Believers get to know who their God is and what that God wants through revelation. Judaism is one of the religions classified as "Revealed Religion," a type that challenges the atheist allegation that religion is merely a "figment of the imagination." Rather, Judaism (and other revealed religions) demonstrate that religion is "a human response" to Divine initiative. Also, Judaism presents the reader with the example that God calls for purpose - those God calls are challenged to carry out a mission to the world. This is why the sacred book of Judaism conveys doctrine - teaching that is good not only for the Jews, but also for the whole world. The following statements express central aspects of Judaism.

I. Shema

Deuteronomy 6:4-9 is a very special passage in the Torah whose main purpose is to direct Jews to Judaism. The commandments teach monotheism. "Hear, O Israel! The Lord is our God, the Lord alone. You shall love the Lord your God with all your heart and with all your soul and with all your might. . . " (Deut. 6:4f).

1. The Shema: (that God - their God - is not only the Creator of the whole universe, but is also its ruler - that God is worthy of worship because God is the Lord of the Universe, *Deut. 6;4*).
2. That God is spirit and those who worship God must do so in spirit and in truth.
3. That God gave humanity freedom (free will) to either commit themselves to God or die by separating themselves from the source of life.
4. That humanity can make the decision either to do good; i.e., God's will, or to commit evil deeds; i.e.., sin.
5. That a human being is created good, in God's image, but is often susceptible to sin.
6. That those who sin will be punished on the judgment day. Those who do God's will, though they die, yet they will resurrect from the dead and live eternally with God who is Everlasting.
7. That the Messiah shall come to set in motion the Kingdom of God; i.e., peace, eternity, and goodness.

ii. A Theology of Judaism

Judaism has two creeds: 1) the Shema, which describes a daily prayer which every adherent of Judaism observes; and 2) the thirteen principles of belief. According to Deuteronomy 6:4-5, Jewish doctrine of God is clear. Theirs is an unquestionable monotheism, requiring adherents to worship God with "all their heart, soul and might." Only God is worthy of worship. The Jewish view of God is clearly distinct from Christian Trinitarian theology. Jewish theology holds that God is transcendent, which means that God is believed to be eternal, incorporeal, incomparable, omnipresent, omniscient, immutable and omnipotent. Although Jewish theology teaches that God is incorporeal, it still uses anthropomorphic language. God hears, sees, feels, speaks and "walks in the cool of the day." However, no matter what can be said about God, Jewish theology teaches that God is incapable of being fully comprehended by the human mind. God is also imminent. God's Shekhinah (indwelling presence) fills the whole universe - heaven and earth. One becomes conscious of the Shekhinah in such happenings as "the burning bush" (Exodus 3:15). Jewish theology talks in terms of God being "present" in the written word (The Torah), in the Temple, in prayer and in acts of mercy and justice.

On the other hand, the presence of the Lord cannot be experienced in an evil setting. Acts of murder, immorality and the like are incompatible with the presence of God. Evil obscures the holy presence; otherwise, God is omnipresent. Although terms and concepts like "the house of the Lord' are used, they do not signify "housing God" because such is an impossibility.

God is also thought of as "personal." God's holy name is YHWH. Though personal, God is believed to be eternal. Note that although Jewish theology generally uses male metaphor to describe God, there are also female metaphors such as in Isaiah 66:13 where God is viewed as a mother comforting her child. According to some sources, "The Shekhinah (God's indwelling presence) is the female aspect of God" (Patterns of religion 1999, 448).

Jewish theology is never complete unless these four personal characteristics are expressed: creator, redeemer/deliver, revealer, and king/judge. Genesis makes it clear that, according to Judaic theology, it is God alone who brought everything into being. There is nothing that was created which was not created by YHWH. Further, everything created was brought into being by God and therefore is good. All creation is good.

In Jewish theology, God reveals Godself to humanity. God's will is made known to God's people. God speaks to humanity through the prophets and any other forms determined by YHWH to be appropriate. Humanity is charged with obedience, faithfulness and complete trusting surrender. However, humanity, like all creation, falls short of the glory of God. Jewish theology teaches that unless God sends deliverance, humanity will eventually perish. God also speaks to the Jew through mediums such as the Torah where God's law is laid out. Humanity must always repent, obey God and receive God's deliverance. Finally, God or YHWH is the ultimate judge. In Jewish theology, goodness is rewarded, sinful acts are punished. All rests with God.

d.   *Zionism: Judaic Ideology*

The origin of Zionism can be traced back to a general phenomenon that Jews prosper wherever they go, yet they are a people without a homeland. The term "Zionism" is commonly defined as "the movement to establish a Jewish homeland in a particular geographical location. A negative attitude toward Jews is generally described as anti-Semitism, a term which would be the opposite of Zionism. Put differently, one could say Zionism is a two-pronged movement: 1) a movement toward establishing a homeland for the Jews so that they are not viewed as aliens wherever they are, and 2) movement to not only resist but fight the anti-Semitic attitudes in the world. Since one does not have to be an adherent of Judaism to promote Zionism, this movement is not to be equated with Judaism. For instance, one of the leading proponents, if not founder of Zionism, was a marginal Jewish practitioner. Theodor Herzl, a liberal Jew had little or no interest in the Jewish religion, but nation. "Herzl urged Jews to establish their own state. He was instrumental in organizing the first Zionist Congress, which was held in Basel, Switzerland, in August 1897, and which sought an international charter for a Jewish homeland" (Patterns of Religion 1999, 485).

This movement encouraged Jews to immigrate to the land of Palestine. Sources indicate and agree that of the approximately 40,000 Zionist who immigrated to Palestine, more than half the population were socialists who were committed to "a classless society." Within a few decades (by 1914), there were almost a hundred thousand Jews in Palestine. Many established agricultural communities (known as Kibbutz). Through the efforts of people like the president of the World Zionist Organization (Chaim Weizmann) and the British Foreign Office, The British government endorsed and committed itself to the establishment of the Jewish homeland in Palestine. Later, the league of Nations adopted this position, giving Britain the mandate to govern Palestine, with view to lead them to political independence. In 1948, Israel became a sovereign state.

As the Jews were preparing themselves for sovereign status, they found themselves divided over what kind of a sovereign state they wanted to be. On the one hand, the religious Jews wanted to resume a theocracy (government by God), on the other hand, secure Zionist Jews preferred a secular democratic state. Jews of socialist persuasion preferred a secular, socialist democratic state. This faction was largely responsible for the creation of the Kibbutz Community Concept.

Zionism was viewed by some as another form of Judaism - defined not by the covenant with God, but with culture and commitment to the homeland. For factional leaders like Ahad Ha-Am, Zionism was Judaism. Further, as far as the secular Jews were concerned, being a Jew did not depend on "obedience to God" as had been the history of Israel. Rather, the issue of identity was resolved "by insisting that Jews are Jews by birth and heritage," rather than by obedience to God' (Patterns of Religion 1999, 485).

e. *Humanity and Morality*

The Jewish community has had periods of extreme oppression since its inception! The most conspicuous incidents are the enslavement in Egypt, the Babylonian rule and the holocaust. But when the Jews remember situations like the "Passover", they feel empowered and assured that truly God is faithful and just. They can rely on God for deliverance. Also, such memories do not only strengthen their membership as a community but they also give character to their membership. This is why for the longest time, the Jews simply referred to themselves as "a people of faith". Further, the Jews also thought of themselves as a "chosen people" although they believe that their Yahweh is the Lord of the whole universe. Yahweh is the Creator and Ruler of the whole world, according to biblical sources like Deuteronomy.

So, how does Israel become "a chosen people"? The answer is simple: Israel responded to God's covenant and therefore Israel will receive the blessings that God promised those who respond to the Divine offer. This, however, does not mean that Israel can disobey God and get away with it. To the contrary, God has placed a very high standard on Israel's morality. In fact, God has given them a code of ethics to live by.

This is why many scholars do not interpret the phrase "a chosen people" to be exclusive. God is the universal God who rules the whole world with power, justice and grace.

The guiding principles of Jewish morality are spelled out in the Torah. Israel has accepted them as their moral ideals. However, incidents like the holocaust have caused Jewish people to wrestle with a more contemporary meaning of "a chosen people". According to Matthews, "In medieval Judaism, Judah Halevi advanced the idea that from the time of Adam, Jewish people were endowed with a special religious faculty" (Matthews 1999, 320). Other Jews have now developed the theory that "Judaism is identical with a religion of reason" (Matthews 1999, 320). One question that always looms at the surface is: does being a chosen people bring suffering along with the blessings? Viewed from another angle, however, the concept of a chosen people could be treated as a common characteristic of most religions. Any people with a particular religion are likely to develop a concept like that. Their God/deity is theirs. The deity promises them "good things" and the people seek to please their God. With this interpretation, one may get a new understanding of the "chosen people" concept. To some, the concept ceases to be exclusivistic, rather it becomes "characteristic of a passionately religious people". This is also true of even non-theistic religions like Buddhism. Devotees claim ownership of the Enlightenment ideal. Yet, in each case, we are to understand that particularism of originality need not confine a religion to exclusivism. In the case of Judaism, there is always a very healthy tension between such particularity and the religion's universal vision. A similar type of tension can be detected in Israel's pride and her humility as "a chosen people". At the end of the day, Israel as a community of the chosen people "thinks in terms of a community chosen to be repsonsible to God" (Matthews 1999, 320), who is the ruler of the universe!

Righteousness, defined as being in right relationship with God and one's neighbor, is supreme in Jewish morality. The Jew has ethical duties toward God as well as toward one's fellow human being, regardless of race or nationality. Ethics is the essence of Judaism. Together, being ethical and theological results in being holy. Scriptures, such as Leviticus 19:2, raise the standard of holiness to the level of Deity: ***"Since humanity was created in the image of God, humanity is challenged to comply with what God has legislated through the Pentateuch written by Moses."***

A statement that constitutes the core of morality is summarized in the book of Exodus 34:6-7: ***"The Lord, God is merciufl and gracious, slow to anger, and abounding in steadfast love and faithfulness, keeping*** *steadfast love for thousands, forgiving iniquity and transgression and sin."* God has already defined what is good in the Pentateuch. For instance, Leviticus 19:18 summarizes the whole concept of morality: *"Love your neighbor as yourself."* Indeed, it could be said that biblical morality was inteded by the author to help all humanity to live in harmony, although specific instructions have been directed toward the Jews. For in the whole world, if "we loved our neighbor as we loved ourselves," this world would be a true community of humanity.

Kosher Laws

Based on scriptures like Leviticus 11:1-47 and Deuteronomy 14:3-20, Judaism has developed Kosher laws which all-obserrvant Jews are expected to comply with. Kosher laws govern birds, fishes, and mammals that are regarded as clean and fit for human consumption. God's law stipulates that Jews are permitted to eat animals that "chew the cud" such as cattle, sheep, and goats. Also, these animals are kosher provided that they, in addition to being cud-chewing, have cloven hooves. Those without these two features such as rabbits, camels, and its are forbidden. Although they are God's creation, they are unclean. In the waters, only those with fins and scales are kosher. In the air, scavenger birds are non-kosher.

Obedience to the Torah

Judaism teaches that, while sacrifices are important, obedience to God's, moral commands and deeds of love were preferrable. Most of the biblical mitzvot are moral directives, for example: Observe the Sabbath Day and keep it holy. Don't commit murder, adultery, etc. You shall not oppress the widow or the orphans. Do not accept bribes. Do not deny charity to the poor. Do not administer capital punishment based on a majority of one. However, Judaism respects life so much that in critical situations when it becomes a question of "saving a life" or "observing the Sabbath", Judaism teaches that the former takes precedence. This also leads to certain virtues.

Basic Judaic virtues are such attributes as justice and mercy. Jews are commanded to love all human beings and lead them to the Torah, i.e., obedience to God. Jews are to learn from God's examples. For instance, Yahweh is merciful, loving and compassionate. So must they be. In fact, according to one well-respected Rabbi (Akiva ben Josef) of the first centrury, "...the failure to do so is analogous to murder". The ethical legacy of Judaism consists of engaging in the struggle for civil rights, racial equality and economic justice. According to Hillel the Elder, "the Golden Rule is the basic principle underlying God's laws: What is hateful to yourself, do not do to your neighbor. This is the whole Torah; the rest is commentary" (Shabbbat 31a). In sum, Judaic ethic is one of obedience. Obedience to the Tora (God's law) will save Israel.

Topics for Discussion

1. Discuss the causes of racism in light of the holocaust.

2. Discuss Jewish morality vis-a-vis the evil of racism.

3. What is the role of *prophecy* in Jewish faith, economics, history and politics?

4. Discuss Zionism as a political concept.

5. Discuss the concept of a "calling".

6. Discuss various Jewish holidays and their "historical/religious" significance.

7. Discuss: why did God seem to have favored the Jews? (Egyptians and Canaanites)?

8. Discuss the concept of child abuse with reference to Joseph, Isaac, and Ishmael in the bible.

Chapter 7

Christianity

The Background of Christianity

Christianity shares ancestry with Judaism because the former emerged from the latter. Christian concepts of revelation, God, sin, creation, salvation, humanity, and heaven, to mention a few, are similar to those of Judaism. It is therefore not surprising that much of Christian faith is actually based on Jewish sacred books (Old Testament) hence the term Judao-Christian tradition. Of course the difference is that what Christians regard as the "Old" is the Jewish current scriptures. However, even what Christians call the "New" Testament is itself replete with references and quotations from the Jewish bible. Consequently, one can summarize the whole scenario this way: Christianity, which started about 2,000 years ago, has its ancestry in Judaism, which began about 4,000 years ago, and both religions are counted among the revealed religions of the world. Also, both are monotheistic although one is Christocentric and the other is Theocentric.

The Patriarchs

The rationale for beginning the history of Christianity with a quick excursion of Jewish history is that the founder of Christianity and most of the authors of the scriptures (both the Old and the New Testaments), are Jews; the context is such that it is almost mandatory that one begins with Judaism.

According to the Jews, God established a <u>covenant</u> with Abraham

(Genesis 12:1-3), a contractual agreement which became the basis for not only Judaism but Jewish nationalism over 4000 year ago. In essence, the covenant consists of God's promise to bless Abraham and his descendants; and Abraham's pledge to faithfulness to God. Differently put, God said: I will be your God if you will be faithful to me. Abraham decided that all his male descendants would be circumcised to memorialize the covenant.

Ever since, any time the Jews prospered, credit was given to their God; any disaster such as disease or military defeat was understood to be God's punishment for some misdeeds. With reference to identity, Abraham's descendants were originally known as Hebrews, but at some point (Genesis 32:22-32), Jacob was renamed "Israel" which means "he who strives with God." This Peniel incident led Abraham's people to be renamed Israelites. Jacob's twelve sons constituted the twelve tribes of Israel.

Following a major regional famine the Israelites migrated to Egypt in search of grain. Eventually, however, the Israelites were enslaved by the Egyptians for about 400 years after which God empowered Moses to liberate the people of Israel from bondage (about 13 Century B.C.E.). Again, credit for the liberation was given to God. The covenant between God and the people was renewed and God gave them the Ten Commandments to observe. This decalogue (Exodus 20:3-17) given at Mt. Sinai has become a major moral bond between God and Israel. Christians have also adopted the Ten Commandments, believing that observing these is being faithful to God who blesses the Faithful and punishes those who disobey his law.

Political Structure

The people of Israel accepted the political rule of God. Their government is generally referred to as a theocracy-, which means "Government by God." Following Moses' leadership out of Egypt, Joshua led the nation in conquering the Canaanites, believing that that was the land where God wanted them to settle, hence the designation: The Promised land.

Hereafter, the twelve tribes had the tradition of being "ruled" by a judge. This lasted from about 210 B.C.E. to 1020 B.C.E. Eventually, the idea of being ruled by judges was replaced by the concept of royalty (about 1020 to 922 B.C.E.). Thus, God appointed Saul (in 1021-1000 B.C.E.) to be the first king of Israel. After him came King David (1000-961 B.C.E). Both kings had to fight with the Philistines. By the time

Solomon was king, Israel had been fairly well established in the Middle East region. Remembering the covenant between God and themselves, King Solomon was the first to build a temple in the city of Jerusalem.

Upon Solomon's death, the Kingdom of Israel experienced schism. Ten tribes to the north named themselves Israel while the remaining two to the south assumed the name Judah (from 922-722 B.C.E.). The nation was destroyed by Assyria. Throughout, Israel kept a constant dialogue with God via the vehicle of the prophets. Major figures in this regard included the prophets Elijah, Elisha, Isaiah, Jeremiah and Ezekiel to mention a few. The purpose of these prophets was generally "to speak for God" - they told Israel what God was saying. Major themes the prophets introduced included:

1. that true religion is grounded in ethics;
2. that true religious practitioners cannot mistreat other human beings;
3. that true religion involve having a pure heart;
4. that true religion is being God's witness to the nations of the world.

This message to Israel is based on the assumption that Israel is "the Chosen nation" - chosen to witness God's word to the whole world.

The name "Judaism" emerged following the destruction of the northern kingdom (Israel), and the survival of the southern kingdom of Juda. Later, Judah was captured by the Babylonians (from 722 B.C.E. to 538 B.C.E.) when God later redeemed them by sending Cyrus, a Persian king to defeat the Babylonians and set the Jews at liberty to return to their Promised Land. While in captivity, Israel always hoped that God would send the Messiah to liberate them.

Jesus of Nazareth

Following many years of Israel's oppression and domination by other powers like the Babylonians, the Persians, the Greeks, and the Romans, the people of Israel became very frustrated. They began to wonder why "the chosen" people were experiencing so much political domination. It was during this time that the concept of a messiah whom God would send to deliver them developed and was regarded as their salvation. Jesus the Christ, therefore, was assumed to be the one to deliver Israel from its political suffering, if he was the Christ! And when Jesus said: "The Kingdom of God is at hand", the Jews were really hopeful that "this is the Day of the Lord." Their deliverance was at hand! But Jesus turned out to be a different kind of a deliverer.

Jewish Factions

At the time Jesus appeared, Israel had at least four major factions: the Zealots, the Essenes, the Pharisees, and the Sadducees. A brief description of each will suffice.

a.   The Zealots:

This group was involved in Jewish Society. It was an underground party plotting to overthrow Rome. The Zealots expected Christ to lead them to victory over their oppressors. Unfortunately that was not what Jesus Christ was about.

b.   The Essenes:

The Essenes consisted of a militant group which rejected Greek rule. Rather than attack the Greek leaders, they chose to retreat to the desert and lived in communes. While waiting for the Messiah to overthrow Rome, the Essenes engaged in strict study of the Law (i.e. the Bible). They were preparing themselves to be the true Israel God would use to put in place the New Covenant.

The remaining two groups were more conspicuous - The Pharisees and the Sadducees.

c.   The Sadducees:

The Sadducees were the wealthy ruling party. Among them were the high priests who played a major role in the nation's governing body (the Sanhedrin). The Sadducees taught very strict observance of the Torah. They were much more conservative than other groups, certainly more than their main internal opponent, the Pharisees. They believed in maintaining the Law of Moses as it was given by Yahweh at Mt. Sinai. For instance, any new interpretations of the Torah were rejected because they were regarded as a departure from the truth. Sadducees rejected new ideas about life after death, spirits, angeology, pneumatology and the resurrection of the body. Politically, Sadducees tended to cooperate with

d. The Pharisees:

The Pharisees were basically liberal minded. Among them were largely merchants and artisans who actively sought to preserve Jewish cultural and religious purity. Unlike the Sadducees, Pharisees were open to the oral interpretation of the Law for the purpose of applying it to their daily life. For instance, they accepted the theology of life after death as well as the idea of the resurrection of the body. For the Pharisees, Messiahnism, was more spiritual than merely political. However, like the other groups, except the Sadducees, the Pharisees rejected the concept of foreign rule. One other difference between these two groups was that Pharisees made Judaism more accessible to the public than did the temple-centered Sadducees..

In sum, some of the most important ideas in Christianity certainly grew out of Judaism. Himself a Jew, there is no doubt that Jesus drew substantial data, concepts and theology from his Jewish heritage. It is interesting to note that the Jews decided to crucify Jesus who had come to the world to die for the salvation of all creation. Did Jesus have to be crucified by "the chosen nation?" Were the Jews chosen to be the ones to crucify Christ?

The Life of the Founder

Christianity was founded by a Jew by the name of Jesus who became known as the Christ. Born in Bethlehem (between 6 BCE and 4:BCE), a small town in Israel, raised in Nazareth - also a small town Jesus grew up in the Pharisaic tradition. This faction of Judaism has traditionally been more liberal than the Sadducees. Having been raised as the son of a carpenter, at 30, Jesus began to publicly preach his radical or untraditional understanding of faith in God. His teachings have been preserved in body of writing generally known as the Gospels, which also serve as Jesus' biography and constituting part of the most sacred literature - the Bible. Although Christianity used both the Tanakh (the Bible for Judaism) and the Gospels, Jesus' central teachings and beliefs are found in the latter. Jesus himself did not write any gospel, but those he taught remembered his teachings.

Mary, a young virgin, is believed to be the mother of Jesus. Regarding the man's father, Christians believe that although Mary was engaged to Joseph, she conceived through the power of the Holy Spirit; i.e., God simply declared that she would be with a baby who would be named Jesus. After getting over the shock, Joseph accepted what had happened to his "bride" and would become Jesus' earthly father, though non-biological. According to the gospels, Jesus actually regarded God as his "Father in Heaven." This obviously made Jesus a rather peculiar individual described in the gospels as:

1. The Son of God
2. The Savior of the whole world
3. The Lamb of God who takes away the sins of the whole world
4. The prince of peace
5. The Christ (meaning the anointed one)
6. God; i.e., fully God and fully human
7. The Messiah

Several other titles were given to Jesus, but these are the more common ones. Jesus called himself "the son of man" on the one hand and he also referred to "MY Father in heaven." So, Jesus is to be understood as to having two natures.

The Distinguishing Character of the Founder

Several distinctive features marked the life or ministry of Jesus. Jesus taught the message of *repentance* because the "Kingdom of God is near" (Mark 1:14-15). It is striking to note that the call to repentance was made to the adherents of Judaism. As had John the Baptist, Jesus called these to be "transformed" and to turn to God who loves and forgives graciously. Jesus showed special concern, almost bordering on showing preference to the marginalized, the poor, the outcasts, the sinner! This was not a common characteristic expected of a Rabbi. Yet this was consistent with his message and presentation of what the love of the gracious God is. Next, all gospels record a series of conflicts between Jesus and the elders of the Synagogue and the Temple based on how they understood the "Law and the Prophets" and how Jesus interpreted the same. Jesus was intentional about this confrontation as portrayed in the formulation, "you have heard it said. . .but I say to you. . ." (Matthew 5:38-42). He also attacked those who presented themselves as "righteous," "Law-abiding" for being self-righteous and arrogant in their religiosity. For Jesus, the Torah meant more than just memorizing the scriptures. The Torah only provided a clue to real morality; namely, loving God - wholeheartedly -

with one's heart, soul and body, and the love of one's neighbor as oneself. Put differently, Jesus insisted on not only orthodoxy but also orthopraxis.

Jesus' ministry and teachings made a special use of the traditional pedagogical employment of the parables. Parables are stories told in order to lead the audience to deeper morality and clearer spiritual insight. Whether it was through the Parables, the beatitudes, or other aspects of the sermon on the mountain, Jesus' teachings presented the listeners with a radical ethic - repentance - a complete turn around. In addition to their radical character, Jesus' teachings were open to anyone - they had no class or gender boundaries.

All this made such an impact on Jesus' contemporaries that resentment, anger and hate mounted in the Jewish community culminating in their resolution to crucify Jesus. Events leading to this death are also recorded in the gospels. Central to this are the following:

1. Jesus was betrayed by one of his disciples, Judas Iscariot, the man who served as the treasurer for the group. He was paid (about 30 pieces of silver) by the Roman soldiers to signal to them who the victim was.
2. Jesus had the Last Supper with his disciples.
3. Jesus was accused of wanting to overthrow the Roman provincial government, an allegation which was supposed to infuriate the Romans. But after the official trial by Pontius Pilate, Jesus was found innocent of any insurrection charges. The Jews really felt that Jesus' alleged claims were an insult to their God and therefore should be hanged. Unfortunately, the Romans had no problem with that type of an offense. So, political allegations were fabricated to appear like "political offenses" which the Romans would not tolerate for one moment. Most scholars concur that Pilate had Jesus crucified to keep the peace with the Jewish leaders.
4. On Friday of His trial week, Jesus was crucified, dead and buried.
5. Jesus was raised from the tomb on the third day - early Sunday morning.
6. Jesus visited with his disciples for a little while, then ascended to heaven, where he sits "on the right hand of God, the Father."
7. Jesus is the founder of Christianity because the "Christian church" worships God through his name as the Christ and the Living God.

Salient Christian Beliefs

Christianity believes in a Trinitarian God, defined as "one but three at once." This unique concept is to be found in Christianity alone.

According to the doctrine of the Trinity, God has a dynamic, personal and relational nature. The Trinity includes God the Father, to whom creation is attributed; God the Son, to whom the redemption or salvation of all creation is attributed; and God the Holy Spirit of comfort, inspiration, teaching and guiding the Church. But scholars have made it clear that to talk of God as "three-in-one" is never to be misconstrued to mean "three Gods." Christianity is unequivocally monotheistic and any language about God has to be understood as merely analogous. When Christians talk about divine nature, specifically about the Trinity, it is to be regarded as merely a confession rather than an explanation because there is an element of mystery in the nature of the Trinity. We have already seen that even the birth of Jesus has been portrayed by tradition as supernatural.

Theologians, over the centuries, have developed some important concepts of who God is. For instance, beyond acknowledging God as the sole creator of the universe, God is perceived as spirit, perfect, love and truth. For the majority of Christian believers, God is the First Principle - the Uncaused Cause. God is the Unmoved Mover who is responsible for everything that has motion and all existence. God is the only "necessary Being" upon whom all is contingent. Put differently, God is the foundation on which every created thing stands and from which it draws its existence. In short, we *are* because God *is*. However, the opposite is not true...God *is* in spite of us. God is not defined by creation.

Most Christian theologians concede that not only was Jesus the Son of God, he was God incarnate. God who is Spirit, became flesh in Jesus and "dwelt among us." He was the ultimate revelation of God the Father. Jesus' major purpose in this world was to reveal the true nature of God; i.e., when we say God is love, we learn what that means from the life and teachings of Jesus. When we say God is a caring God, we can see how that is enacted in the life and ministry of Jesus, and so forth.

Christian Doctrine of Humanity

Christianity teaches that humanity was created in the image of God, the Creator. Christianity further teaches that while humanity is "the image of God," it is different from God precisely because creation is *ipso facto* different from its creator. Having said this, we can now proceed to say that God created humanity out of God's own pleasure, not due to necessity. *God did not have to create human beings or any other creature.* God brought into existence human beings because God loves humanity. Thus, Christianity teaches a theocentric view of the cosmos. The religion regards all creation from the point of view that God is the center, the Source, the beginning and end of everything. Therefore, humanity has been described as "children of God." Most Christians do not embrace the evolution theory, although many argue that whatever theory is advanced - including the Big Bang theory - at the very beginning it is God who brought matter into existence.

Christianity also presents humanity as the center of all that was created. The Bible (*Genesis and Psalms*) points out that humanity is a very special creature in the whole universe. Humans are described as being "a little less than the angles" (Psalms 8:5). However there is another view. Christianity also presents humanity as "sinful by nature." Because human beings are "sinful by nature," it is therefore necessary that there be a savior to redeem humanity from sin. On this sbuject many theologians argue convincingly that if humanity is sinful by nature, it cannot necessarily save itself from its own condition. Furthermore, since humanity is "sinful by nature" naturally sins since such is its nature. Thus, sin is a human necessity - it has to be the only human choice. However, the fact that Adam and Eve sinned and "have brought sin into the world" need not make sin a "necessity." The good news is that Jesus came and died on the cross so that all creation may see salvation.

The whole biblical story of Adam and Eve committing the first sin helps Christians to tell the story of how disobeying God's word (or commmands) does strain the relationship between God (the Creator) and humanity. The same story is employed by Christians to explain a theolgoy of the Divine initiative, namely, that God takes the first step to save humanity from sin since it is God who "walked in the cool of the day" and called, "Adam, Adam, where are you?" (Genesis 3:8-10). The coming of Jesus to the world can be logically viewed as God in pursuit of sinful humanity. In telling the story of Adam's sin, those who wrote the Bible make the statement that "all human beings are sinful." If we are all from the loins of Adam, " it follows that to sin is our nature. However, some theologians do not accept this implied consequence or its monogenistic source. They do not subscribe to the theology that all human beings come from "the loins of Adam," therefore they do not buy into the original sin theology. Sin cannot be inherent in humanity. What they argue is that the world into which every human being is born is in a condition which is conducive to sin. The difference between these two perspectives is crucial. It also helps Christians to deal with the theological question, "why do bad things happen to good people?"

Because the world cannot save itself from its own state which is conducive to sin, it is necessary for power - almighty power - to intervene and redeem humanity from such a condition. Christianity teaches about the God of Grace. Therefore, through the "grace of our Lord Jesus Christ," the helpless world will be saved by God the Son, who is the redeemer or Savior of the whole creation.

The Gospel (the good news) Christians preach proclaims that God, through Jesus Christ, will save the world from its sin so that "those who believe this will live eternally." Other major doctrines include forgiveness, love and immortality or resurrection.

The Immortality of the Soul

Although the belief in life after death is held by many religions, Christians base it on the example set by Jesus Christ who, after being dead for three days, was raised from the dead by God. They believe that those who enter eternal life will forever live with God who is eternal. Christian faith recognizes that human beings do not live in this physical form forever. However, after a temporary separation of the body and the spirit, there will be a time when these two re-unite in a "glorious heavenly body" that will live with God forever. Christians generally regard such eternal existence as a form of a reward for having lived a good life on earth. Thus, heaven is the ultimate reward for the good, while hell is the eternal punishment for those who did not live a good life. In many Christian circles, the description of heaven is such that everybody wants or, rather, hopes to enter such a kingdom. By contrast, hell is depicted as a place of torment - eternal suffering which was prepared by God in the beginning of time for those who would live an immoral life.

The Roman Catholic Church has developed a belief that is slightly different from the Protestant Christian view. Their concept of purgatory says that there is a temporary waiting place of punishment and suffering for those who die in sin, though God is still gracious with them. Protestantism does not seem to be very clear on the subject of "heaven and hell." But there is a general belief that when a person dies, the soul/spirit will go to either heaven or hell, depending on God's decision and judgment, based on the deeds of the individual. What is vague is *when* this happens.

Christianity's biggest adversary is personified as the Devil or

Satan. In fact, Satan is presented as one competing with God for "clients" in the world. Those who are spiritually weak are easily won over by the Devil who promises transient pleasures, after which these people will enter eternal hell. Evil and sin are thought of as individual or collective. The evil of racism, for instance, tends to be collective, whereas stealing could be an individual sin. In either case, there is no greater or smaller sin. Sin is sin. The church also realizes although it is "the body of Christ," it does make mistakes in history - it commits sin; such as the sin of omission, commission, etc. But the church will not tolerate any allegations that God sins because God is believed to be the only Perfect One. In connection with this, there has been a theological debate on "theodicy." Christianty belives that God is all-good, all-powerful, all-knowing, and everywhere at once - even though evil is also everywhere in the world. Such evil is not part of God! The hope of Christianity rests upon Jesus' promise that he is with us until the end of age. The theodicial question that arises is, why do bad things happen to good people since Jesus is with them always until the end of the age?

Christian Faith and Practice

Generally speaking, Christian people are those bapitized in the name of the founder of the religion. They therefore intend to follow the example of morality set by Jesus. Central to Christian morality is love for one another as well as love for God. The gospels tell us succinctly, "what I command you is to love one another (John 15:17). Christian love is different from romantic emotions or filial love and love between friends is different from what the Christian love is about. Christian love calls the adherents to be compassionate to all human beings, including one's "enemies" and those "who hate you" (Luke 6:27). This is the love that Jesus demonstrated and, therefore, is what is expected of every Christian. Christian adherents are taught to be in harmony with their neighbor. War is immoral. Christians do not seek vengeance. The watch word for Christians is *love*; that is, selfless love generally referred to by theologians as *agape*, defined as "unconditional love."

Agape is the highest kind of love - perfect love that is unconditional. This is what God's love is. Christians are called upon to be "as perfect as" their God (Matthew 5:48). This is truly a high ideal achieved by God's grace.

Christians believe that every person is endowed with a moral conscience. Every human being has "the regulator" for morality, which summons one either to do good or consciously avoid evil. Human beings are, therefore, responsible for their thoughts and deeds. They are expected to live a moral life. This is more than obeying *The Ten Commandments*. Rather it is to be a way of life. A life of morality is synonymous with being in God's company.

To be a Christian is to live in compliance with God's love as manifested in Jesus Christ, who is the means of grace. Christians participate in certain Holy actions, better known as sacraments, through which and by which they receive God's grace. Generally, the church recognizes seven sacraments; namely, the Eucharist, baptism, extreme unction, penance, holy matrimony, confirmation, and holy orders. However, Protestants generally believe in only two of these - the Euchanist and baptism.

The Roman Catholic Church acknowledges all seven, but the Coptic and the Anglican Churches acknowledge a few more than the two observed by most Protestant Churches.

Christians also believe that the adherent can be in the presence of God through prayer. Prayer lifts one's heart and mind to God in order to experience intimate communication with the God of Love. The majority of Christians simply worship through reciting such prayers as *The Lord's Prayer*, or *The Prayer of Confession*, and so forth. They also pray from their own hearts. Whichever way it is offered, prayer is to be understood as special communion with one's God.

Christian Theology

The Christian doctrine of God (the Trinity) distinguishes this religion from most major monotheistic religions of the world. Christian theology is quite clear that it is not polytheistic. Like Judaism and Islam, Christianity believes in the unicity of God who is also viewed as personal. There is consensus among Christian theologians that as far as this religion is concerned, the primary knowledge of God can only be based on what God has revealed, both about Divine Nature and will. Because of this characteristic, proponents of Christian theology rank Christianity superior to all other revealed religions.

For Christians, the attributes of God include creation and redemption of the whole universe. With specific reference to humanity, God is believed to be the great comforter and inspirer. These three functions: creation, salvation and guidance are executed through the Trinity's Father, Son and Holy Spirit respectively. Further, God is personal, though God is not a human being. Even when "personal" language is used - such as talk, hear, love, changed own mind, he, etc. - we are not to conceive God as corporeal. The human language about God must always and only be understood as analogous. Through and through, Christians talk about and understand God in faith. As spirit, God cannot be seen but from time to time God reveals Divine Glory.

God is believed to be the Uncaused Cause, the First Principle, the unmoved Mover and so forth. God is the cause of all truth and goodness in the universe. Not only is the entire universe brought into being by God, it is also controlled by God. Regarding the nature of God, some Christian theologians tasked themselves to "prove" the existence of God. Whatever they came up with actually served to demonstrate that "God is that than which nothing greater can be conceived" (St. Anselm). God is the Ultimate Being. One theologian has described God as "The Ground of Being" (Paul Tillich). God is also attributed with justice, love, perfection, power, worthiness, holiness, as well as foreknowledge and wisdom. Although some of these attributes have been challenged, many Christians still hold on to them.

Christians also talk about God as man in Jesus Christ who was **born** of the Virgin Mary, **died** under Pontius Pilate and was **raised** from the dead on the third day. It is believed that God was **in** Jesus. Put differently, Jesus is God who became flesh and dwelt among us. Jesus is Immanuel. He is God incarnate, the ultimate revelation of God the Father. In and through Jesus we should see who and what God is: love, mercy, grace, forgiving, power overall nature, all-wise. Further, the gospel according to John makes this point (John 13:45). We can know God (the Father) a little more when we understand Jesus, whose personality was intended to reveal God the Father. Based primarily on what Jesus the Christ taught, Christian teachings emphasize the following themes:

1. Love (God and fellow human being).
2. Forgiveness of sin (both horizontally and vertically).
3. Salvation/redemption (bring to everlasting life).
4. Repentance (turn to God, away from evil).
5. Peace (reconciliation among people, making peace).
6. Faith (trust God in everything).
7. Eternal life (there is life after death).
8. Incarnation (God was in Jesus).

Although not all Christians live according to these themes, these give the religion its general character. However, we cannot judge a religion based on its adherents, but its ideals.

Finally, Christian theology teaches about eternal life. It is believed that those who believe in God through Jesus Christ, even though they die like every body else, they will live eternally with God. Life of unbelief is destined to hell, which God prepared from the beginning of creation. In God's foreknowledge, God knows who will end up in hell or in heaven. Human beings have to exercise their free will. In all this it needs to be said that God's plan to save the whole world lies in God's Son, Jesus Christ, the savior of the world.

Topics for Research

1. How viable is the Christian way of life as a non-violent way of reconciliation? To answer this, compare Dr. King, Jr. with Malcolm X as politicians.

2. Discuss at least four parables of Jesus which teach love is the ultimate ideal.

3. Discuss theodicy. (Why do bad things happen to good people?)

4. Discuss angeology. What is the origin of angels, their nature, function, etc.

5. Discuss the origin of Satan.

6. Are human beings sinful by nature?

7. Discuss what the bible says about sex. (You can choose to focus on homosexuality, marriage, pre-marital sex, beastiality, etc.)

8. Disucss Christian teachings and slavery in North America.

Chapter 8

Islam

General Background

Islam is at once one of the world's largest and youngest major religions. According to some authorities one out of every six human beings in the world is a Muslim - making a total of about one billion adherents. Geographically, Muslims are present in large communities on almost all the continents - especially Asia, Europe and Africa. Islamic culture, as well as religion, is most dominant in the Near East, North and West Africa, Asia, India, Europe, and North and South America. It is interesting to note that not all Arabs are Muslims. In fact, the majority of Muslims are non-Arabic, although Islam originated in what is now Saudi Arabia. Specifically, the religion was conceived and born in the city of Mecca.

It is unthinkable that such a great religious movement was founded by one who started off in life as a mere orphan - illiterate and simple - an individual by the name of Muhammad. Put differently, Muhammad became one of the world's greatest prophets in spite of his most humble beginnings. Contrasted with Jesus, who had at least one father, or Siddhartha whose father was royalty, Muhammad never even saw his father! It seems Allah (God), who chose Muhammad, does not consider one's material assets or social status. Rather, Allah selects a person whose spiritual character is suitable to carry out the Divine Purpose. And, whomever Allah selects will never fail, even if he or she is literally attacked by armies. One cannot help but make the theological inference that Islam has become a great religion because Allah, the Almighty, the Compassionate, destined it to be so. Another interesting observation is that, given the strong tribal and clan orientation of the

Quraysh people, for instance, Islam is now represented in nearly every race, as well as on every continent of the world. One more odd fact is that the city of Mecca, for example, was located in a very poor region, yet, due to its geographical location, it became a major center for trade. By design, this would bring in contact people of all walks of life.

Thus, Mecca's cultural and economic influence would also turn the city into the center for religious activity. Certainly the existence of the Ka'bah in Mecca made that city very prominent. Revenue from the pilgrims and taxes from the merchants all made Mecca a powerful center. When it became the center to which all Muslims face when they say their prayers five times a day, it was as if Mecca was simply meant to be. However, there was to be a major difference between the old, corrupt, immoral Mecca and the sacred city - it would be as the religious headquarters of Islam. Last, but not least, it is ironic that the founder of Islam is a member of the Quraysh tribe that had custody of the "corrupt center." It is as if Allah said, "Muhammad, you know your folks better than anyone else, you go and make them **repent**." One cannot say for sure that Muhammad would have been more readily received or listened to if he had been a perfect stranger to the people of Quraysh. But there is no reason to speculate. The historical facts are that the Qurayshians were especially angered, insulted and challenged to have their own - the least among them - preach a strict monotheism in a religious context that acknowledged at least 360 gods! To advocate the worship of one God in an area that thrived in the indefinite multiplicity of deities was just too daring. Yet, that is what was needed.

Islam makes the point clear that its founder is not to be worshiped. He is not the Son of God. In fact, in Islam, idolatry (shirk) is the worst sin. Only Allah is almighty, compassionate, divine and transcendent. Humility is central - in fact, the term *Islam* actually means "submission" and it also refers to the peace that is attained in submission to the one God. Contrasted to Buddhism, named after Buddha, Christianity so called after Jesus Christ, Confucianism after Confucius, Muslims prefer to refer to their religion as Islam (as defined above) rather than the term sometimes used by some people: Mohammedanism. This would suggest that the religion was formed based on an individual - Muhammad. But such is not the case. The religion is a result of total surrender to Allah, presented in the form of the Revelation. Be that as it may, it is important that we devote some time and space to the founderr of Islam - Muhammad.

The Founder of Islam: Muhammad

Born 570 C.E., Muhammad, the man who would be the "last prophet and messenger of Allah," never saw his father, Abdullah, of the Quraysh tribe. His mother, Aminah, of the Hashimite clan, also died when Muhammad was still a lad. So, he was raised to age six by his grandfather. When the old man died, the boy was handed over to an uncle, Abu Talib, who nurtured him. Abu Talib was to play a major role in Muhammad's survival throughout his "dangerous years" of planting the new religion. Although we do not have a formal autobiography of Muhammad, our next most reliable source is the **Hadith** - a body of originally oral traditions from the first generation of Islam. There is also another set of biographies of the prophet from the first centuries of Islam that describe Muhammad's birth as being surrounded with miraculous and mysterious events. In his youth, Muhammad spent several years as a shepherd boy. At twenty-five, he married Khadijah - a wealthy widow who had employed him earlier on. Tradition has it that his widow was over forty years old when she married the twenty-year old Muhammad. Of the several children they had, only Fatima survived both parents. During his adult life, the prophet spent extended periods of time in meditation while the rich wife catered for all family material needs.

The Revelation: 610 C.E.

One day, in 610 C.E., while deeply engrossed in meditation in a cave on Mt. Hira, the Angel Gabriel delivered to Muhammad a message from Allah. The angel's visit was indeed a great mystery, resulting in the revelations that were later recorded, creating what we have today as the **Quran**. During the month of **Ramadan**, the Islamic month, "the angel instructed Muhammad to recite." The initial revelation experience has been remembered as "The Night of Power and Excellence" in the Islamic tradition. The prophet received a series of revelations throughout his life. These were not enjoyable moments in time. We are told that these were moments of extreme seizure-like discomfort and pain. Be that as it may, Muhammad was inspired, excited and moved each time he received the revelation. However, Muhammad and his wife were not sure what all this was about...was the man bordering on insanity? Was he possessed by the jinn? Just what was it? To resolve these questions and contain the anxiety, the couple consulted a **hanif**; i.e., a devout Christian who held strict belief in one God. Here they were assured that what Muhammad was experiencing was indeed divine revelation.

The central inspiration/revelation was relevant to the worship of one God. Polytheism, which most Meccans were involved in, was wrong. Only **Allah** is the one true God, and Muhammad his prophet. When Muhammad began to teach what had been revealed to him, his first convert was Khadijah, his own wife. To date, she is regarded as the first Muslim convert. Many scholars agree that initially, most converts were the poor and the powerless. This angered his own tribesmen to the point where they literally sought to have him assassinated. But Allah, through human as well as other agents, protected this important prophet until his ordained time was over, which came when Islam was on its way to spread all over the world. Today, Islam is rated as the second largest religion among the major religions of the world.

Organization and Institutions

Wherever the religion of the Muslims was introduced, it provided the basic identity and ideology of the nation, a source of unity and solidarity. As the head of the community, the caliph's authority and leadership were rooted in his claim to be the successor of Muhammad himself. The prophet had put in place an impeccable strandard of administration. Control of the community's entire political, judicial, military and fiscal affairs was in the hands of the caliph. Elected by a select group that would present him to the people for "public acclamation," the caliph was the protector and defender of the Islamic faith. The caliph ensured that the community's solidarity was based on a religious bond rather than tribal lineage. In this tradition, there was no room for nepotism. Election to office was based solely on merit and popularity.

Administration was organized around the holy mosque, which served as the religious and public focal point of the surrounding towns. Each of the conquered towns was governed by an authority who generally was a military commander. Law and order was maintained by garrison towns consisting of law enforcement officials. As a rule, to ensure discipline and domination, the conquered towns were divided into provinces, each of which was administered by a governor. Further, the caliphs appointed an agent who oversaw the taxation mechanism (collection and levying of taxes). On the whole revenue for the state came from the captured territories and taxes, across the board.

Islamic system of taxation took various forms including these two: a) the tithe or wealth tax to benefit the poor a land tax paid by Muslims only; b) the poll tax and tribute, later a land tax, paid by non-Muslims.

Peculiar to Islam is the fact that all religious revenue was owned collected and administered by the state. The disbursement of revenue was managed by the registry at Medina, the traditional administrative center. Payment is based on "priority in accepting Islam." That is, a system of pensions was established and maintained by the registry. As a rule, those close to the prophet Muhammad enjoyed special privileges because of their closeness to Allah through Muhammad.

Although in theory, all Muslims are equal, in practice the Muslim society is divided into four classes:

a. the elites of society (the Arab Muslims)
b. the non-Arab converts to Islam
c. the non-Muslim people of the Book (those who possess a revealed scripture, i.e., Christians and Jews) constituted the wider Islamic community-state.
d. the slaves (only those captured in battle could be held as slaves!)

Note, in early Islam, neither Muslims, Jews nor Christians could be enslaved, even if they were "conquered." One can, therefore, see that religion played an important role in the law, taxation, social organization and government. Apparently, Islam respects the other revealed religions of the Middle East, namely Christianity and Judaism since all three religions basically share the same Patriarchal ancestry. Further, the three revealed religions are clearly monotheistic.

Islamic Theology

The Islamic basic creed simply states: "There is no god but God and Muhammad is the messenger of God," indicating that faith in God and the prophet is the foundation of Islamic religion. In addition to these two components (God and Muhammad), Muslims also believe in previous "prophets" (Abraham, Moses, Jesus, etc.), revealed scriptures, angels and the Day of Judgment. One who accepts these precepts is a munin, one who does not believe is Kafir (a pagan, heathen).

In Islamic faith, the purpose of life is not simply to affirm but to realize God's will. Life's purpose is to actualize and not simply articulate the creed. It is not enough to profess belief in God. One needs to realize the will of God. As judgment will be based primarily on deeds, faith not works; that is faith without works is without merit.

According to the Islamic tradition, Kalam (theology) or discourse emerged from concrete issues that needed to be expatiated. A good example is the Muslim-Christian polemics, or the Kharijite split with Ali. Serious theological discussion began during the early caliphal period when several organizational and doctrinal issues had to be discussed. Further, the penetration of Greek philosophy during the Abbasid period was occasion for the development of Islamic theology. In addition, theology was created during the early period when the science of divine unity was constructed and employed as an Islamic discipline. Kalam deliberately mixes politics and faith. Life involves belief, sin, legitimate governance, eschatology, to mention a few major themes. Life is wholistic.

Other key theological issues include: the question of predestination, free will, the nature of God and the Quran, which itself is a major source of theology. Apparently, according to an Islamic theological view, there is a clear need to deal with the relationship of faith to deeds. To be Muslim, one has to be a true believer, or else one is not Muslim. "Complete trusting surrender" means just that. There cannot be middle ground. This sets the scenario for the Islamic worldview, which is dialectic. According to Islamic Kalam, the human community consists of only two categories: believers and infidels. Note that according to this thought, even a person who held as high an administrative position as caliph could become an infidel if he sinned against God, thereby becoming an enemy of Allah just like the rest of the unbelievers in the world. Thus, theologically speaking, one can only retain good standing as a Muslim if one's works are good.

As far as the Kharijites are concerned, even a person closely related to the prophet like Ali (husband of Fatima, the prophet's daughter) had to be "unmuslimized" when he was deemed sinful. Against infidels and illegitimate rulers and renegade Muslims, jihad was mandatory. However, this thinking represents the extremist faction - the Kharijites. The majority of the community did not embrace this degree of extremism. The populous thinking was that only God will judge sinners on the Judgment Day. God alone had the authority and power to exclude a person from Paradise. Based on this theology, mainstream Islam holds the thinking that faith (and just specific works) determined membership in the community, i.e., Islamic family. This allowed (ordinary) sinners to remain in the Ummum. But of course obvious apostasy was "unmuslimized." In Islamic faith it is important to identify the unbelievers not in order to ostracize them but so that the object of Islam's universal mission may be fulfilled - namely to call "all humanity to the worship and service of the one true God" (Esposito, Islam: The Straight Path, 1998, 70).

Islamic theology of predetermination argues, for instance, that because leaders (caliphs) ruled by divine decree, even if they sin, no one can really "unmuslimize" them because their authority was predetermined by God. Regarding themes of predeterminism and free will, Muslims wrestled with the issue of whether God would, in his omniscience, determine a ruler who would sin against Him. Or, it is that God determines a ruler who is obviously human and is free to make choices - right or wrong. Theologically speaking, there cannot be judgment if there is no free will.

Those who believe in free will theology argue that if human beings have free will, they can easily act against what God has predetermined for them. To the contrary, the advocates of determinism contend that if human beings cannot exercise free will, then why would they be judged on the Last Day? It must be that we have free will - to choose to do good or evil and face the consequences. Faced with no easy solution to this dialectic, the majority accept a divinely determined universe. Chief exponents of this theology is the Mutazila movement, an organization which would be interesting to discuss here but time an space do not allow us as we must proceed to discussing the Law.

Islamic Law

The primary religious science in Islam is the Law. Every adherent ought to ask himself or herself the question: what ought I to do? What is Allah's will? In Islamic thought, Law is essentially religious. One can assure oneself that he or she is in the right path (Sharia) if one obeys the Law of God. In fact, all humanity is advised to observe the Law. The law is central to Islamic identity and practice because there is peace, happiness and orderliness in society when everyone observes the Law. This is true irrespective of cultural diversity across the globe. In fact, the Law provides a unifying thread which in turn serves as the point of identity. Because of the centrality of the Law in Islamic society, the Law will always be religiously guarded in the Islamic community. By way of comparison, indeed it could be mentioned that the law in Islam compares to what the Ten Commandments represent in Judaism. In both "religious civilizations" the Law is the life and the faith because its sources are sacred.

The Sources of the Law

Sharia in Islam means literally "the road to the watering hole," meaning the straight path one should follow. Because being Muslim involves "complete trusting surrender to Allah," to be a good Muslim one must believe that the Islamic Law was instituted and mandated by God. For most Muslims, God's will is viewed as synonymous with the Law which is believed to originate from God. Relative to the sources of the Law, since the Quran is not a comprehensive source of the Law, Muslims resorted to developing jurisprudence (i.e., the science of Law). Fi<u>gh</u>, which means "the science of law," is the science that seeks to ascertain, interpret and apply to life the will of God (Sharia) as it is stated in the Holy Quran. In this regard, Islam recognizes four official sources, although there are other less important ones. These are: 1) the Quran; 2) the Sunna of the prophet; 3) the analogical reasoning; and 4) consensus of the community.

1. The Quran

Islamic principles and values are to be found in God's holy book - the Quran which is the record of God's revelation. However, one must always bear in mind that the Quran merely gives broad, general, moral directives of what a Muslim ought to do. In some cases Arab customs have had to be replaced with Islamic standards. Regarding humanizing morality, the Quran discourages for instances, owning slaves, because slavery prevents the individual from achieving their fullest potential as a human being created for a specific purpose. Likewise, women are not to be deprived of their full humanity on account of gender. Women and the family were the subjects of more wide ranging reforms affecting marriage, inheritance and divorce. Polygamy was restricted (4.3); men were required to treat their wives with fairness and equality because they too are God's people created for a purpose. In sum, Quran is a major source of God's word, will and power.

2. The Sunna of the Prophet

Islamic injunctions such as "obey God an obey the messenger" compel everyone to look up to the prophet. Muhammad is the model accepted by good Muslims because there was belief that he was inspired by God to always conduct himself wisely, following God's will. Thus, the

Sunna is held as one of the major sources of the Islamic Law. Consequently, what the prophet did and said became a very important source of the Law. The prophet's biography (the hadith), provided much guidance to the thinking of the Islamic community because it was assumed that the prophet was divinely inspired. Of special importance, however, are the six collections which came to be accepted as authoritative, namely a) those of Ismail al-bukhari, b) Muslim ibn al-hajjaj, c) Abu Dawud, d) al-Nisai, e) al-Tirmidhi, and f) Ibn Maja. Among these, the most popular are the collections of al-Bukhari and the Muslim ibn al-Hajjaj.

3. *The Analogical Reasoning (ijtihad)*

Islamic leaders - caliphs, judges, jurists and legal scholars - had to interpret the law where there was no clear text or consensus. When faced with a new problem, thinkers sought a similar situation in the holy book as well as in the Sunna. Once they discovered reason behind a Sharia rule, they would apply that reasoning to the new problem confronting them. For instance, jurists saw a similarity between the bride's loss of virginity in marriage and the Quranic penalty for theft, which was amputation. Therefore, minimum dower was set at the same rate that stolen goods had to be worth before amputation was applicable. Islamic principle at work here is justice to all. Reason, therefore, is another important source of the Law. The fourth and final source is noteworthy in this discussion: Consensus of the Community.

4. *The Consensus of the Community (ijma)*

Based on the prophet's saying: "My community will never agree on an error," Muslims regard the consensus of the community as a critical source of Law. This source is used in many societies where the majority opinion tends to be accepted as right. Certainly the expression: "majority rules" must have derived from the observation that somehow truth is planted in the hearts of many, if only we are resourceful enough to glean such truth. Over a period of time, Muslims came to identify and recognize two kinds of consensus: a) consensus of the whole community, which was generally applied to such religious duties as the pilgrimage to Mecca; and b) consensus of the community of legal scholars (or religious authority) who ordinarily act in half of the rest of the Muslim community.

In the development of the Islamic Law, one can readily appreciate that the critical role played by consensus of the community would give a letter and more lasting judgment. This applied even to questions on the meaning of parts of the Quran. Generally, most scholars tend to agree with the thinking that consensus of the community, usually endures the test of time. Hence, consensus of the community is a major source of the Law.

By general consensus, most scholars concur with the view that the basic Islamic law was completed by about the tenth century of the common era. The essential principles of the Law had been satisfactorily and comprehensively delineated. On the whole we note that although there is relative harmony within the Islamic community, there still are some differences of opinion, which the prophet always regarded as healthy when he repeated this utterance: "Difference of opinion within my community is a sign of the bounty of Allah."

The Law is administered and applied by the Sharia courts and their judges appointed by the caliph. Believed to be God's Law for the entire Islamic community and indeed for all humanity, the Sharia is in a sense universal and egalitarian. Since the Law answers every Muslims question: what ought I to do or not to do, all acts ought to be regarded as having an ethical dimension, categorized as: 1) obligatory; 2) recommended; 3) indifferent or permissible; 4) reprehensible but not forbidden; or 5) forbidden. For the Muslim, breaking the Law is a serious transgression against both God and society. Offenders will face judgment on the Last Day.

Topics for Research

1. Discuss the rights of women in Islam.

2. Discuss Islamic social impact of the American society today.

3. Discuss the meaning/function of the community in Islam religion.

4. Discuss Islamic laws of property inheritance.

5. Compare Jesus' youth to Muhammad's with specific reference to parentage and identity.

Common Traits	Religion	
	African Religion Christianity Judaism Islam Greek God-Concept	Buddhism (Early Stage) Hinayana Buddhism
1. Belief in God (Supernatural Being)	Yes	None
2. Belief in a superior, intelligent being(s)	Yes	None
3. Deep, intense concern	Yes	Yes
4. Comples worldview interpreting the significance of human life	Yes	Yes
5. Institutionalized social sharing	Yes	Yes
6. Belief in experience after death	Yes	Yes
7. Religious experience after death	Yes	Yes
8. Moral code/code of ethics	Yes	Yes
9. An account of the nature of origin of, and cure for evil	Yes	Yes
10. Prayer and ritual	Yes	Yes
11. Sacred objects and places	Yes	Yes

12. Revealed truths	Yes	Yes/No
Hinduism	Humanism Pantheism	Success, Wealth, Golf, Fishing (Materialism)
Yes	None	None
Yes	None	None
Yes	Yes	Yes
Yes	Yes	Yes
Yes	None	None
Yes	None	None
Yes	None	None
Yes	Yes/None	None
Yes	Yes	None
Yes	None	None
Yes	None	None
Yes	None	None

Appendix V

Research Exercise

The student may earn extra credit by submitting the definition of the following terms regularly during the semester, say in clusters of ten or fifteen.

Agape	bhakti
Allah	Blasphemy
almsgiving	blessed trinity
anicca	bodhisattva
anointing of the sick	born-again
anthrocentricity	Brahma
anthropomorphic	Brahman
anti-semitism	Brahman-atman
apostles	Brahmins
arafat	Buddha
ark	Buddahood
artha	Buddhism
Aryans	Catechumens
Asceticism	Charismatics
atman	Christ
baptism	Communion of Saints
beatitudes	Concupiscence

berakhah

dalit

dependent co-origination

Dhamma

diaspora

Divine Liturgy

docetism

dogma

dukkha

Easter

Ecumenism

episcopacy

Eucharist

Exodus

expedient means

Four Noble Truths

Gospels

grace

guru

hadith

hajj

Crucifix

henotheism

heresy

heterodoxy

hijra

holocaust

humanism

Iblis

icons

ijma

imam

indulgences

inerrancy

infallible

jati

jinn

jnana

justification

Ka'ba

Kama

Karma

Hasids	Khalifa
Hebrew Bible	Kibbutz
kosher	orthodoxy
Kshatriyas	orthopraxis
Laws of Manu	Parable
Lent	Paradigm
magga	paramita
magisterium	Pentacostals
Mahayana Buddhist	Pentateuch
messiah	Pesah
midrash	Pontius Pilate
moksha	Prajnaparamita
monism	Prophecy
monotheism	prophesy
muezzin	Pure Land
muslim	puratory
myth	Purusha
nevi'im	Quran
New Testament	Quraysh
Nibbana (nirvana)	rabbi
numinous	Ramadan

observational meditation

Old Testament

original sin

Salam

Salat

Samsara

Sannyasin

Santi

Satan

Satori

Shahadah

Shahom

Shariah

Shekhinah

Shema

Shiite Islam

Shira

Shirk

Shruti

Shudra

shunyata (emptiness)

reconciliation

Sabbath

Sacrament

Sufis

Sura

synagogue

Synoptic gospels

Talmud

Tanakh

taqwa

tefillin

Theocentricity

theodicy

theophany

Theravada

Theravada Buddhist

tithe

Torah

transcendent

Trinity

tritheism

www.ingramcontent.com/pod-product-compliance
Lightning Source LLC
Chambersburg PA
CBHW050838160426
43192CB00011B/2077